GRAPHIC FORENSIC SCIENCE

SOLVING CRIMES THROUGH
CRIMINAL PROFILING

by Rob Shone

illustrated by Nick Spender

rosen publishing's
rosen central

New York

Published in 2008 by The Rosen Publishing Group, Inc.
29 East 21st Street, New York, NY 10010

First edition, 2008

Designed and produced by
David West Books

Editor: Gail Bushnell

Photo credits:
P4/5, istockphoto.com/Bart Broek; 6t, istockphoto.com/Pascal Le Brun; 7b, istockphoto.com/Lars Christensen; 45, Marlene Thompson/Department of Defense.

Library of Congress Cataloging-in-Publication Data

Shone, Rob.
  Solving crimes through criminal profiling / by Rob Shone ;
illustrated by Nick Spender. -- 1st ed.
      p. cm. -- (Graphic forensic science)
  Includes index.
  ISBN 978-1-4042-1437-8 (library binding) -- ISBN 978-1-4042-1438-5
(pbk.) -- ISBN 978-1-4042-1439-2 (6 pack)
  1. Criminal behavior, Prediction of--Juvenile literature. 2.
Criminal psychology--Juvenile literature. I. Spender, Nik, ill. II.
Title.
  HV6027.S46 2008
  363.25'8--dc22

                        2007044929

This book is produced using paper that is made from wood grown in managed, sustainable forests. It is natural renewable and recyclable. The logging and manufacturing processes conform to the environmental regulations of the country of origin.

Manufactured in China

CONTENTS

RE-CREATING THE CRIME

Collecting the evidence from a crime is important. Understanding that evidence is vital if the culprit is to be caught and convicted.

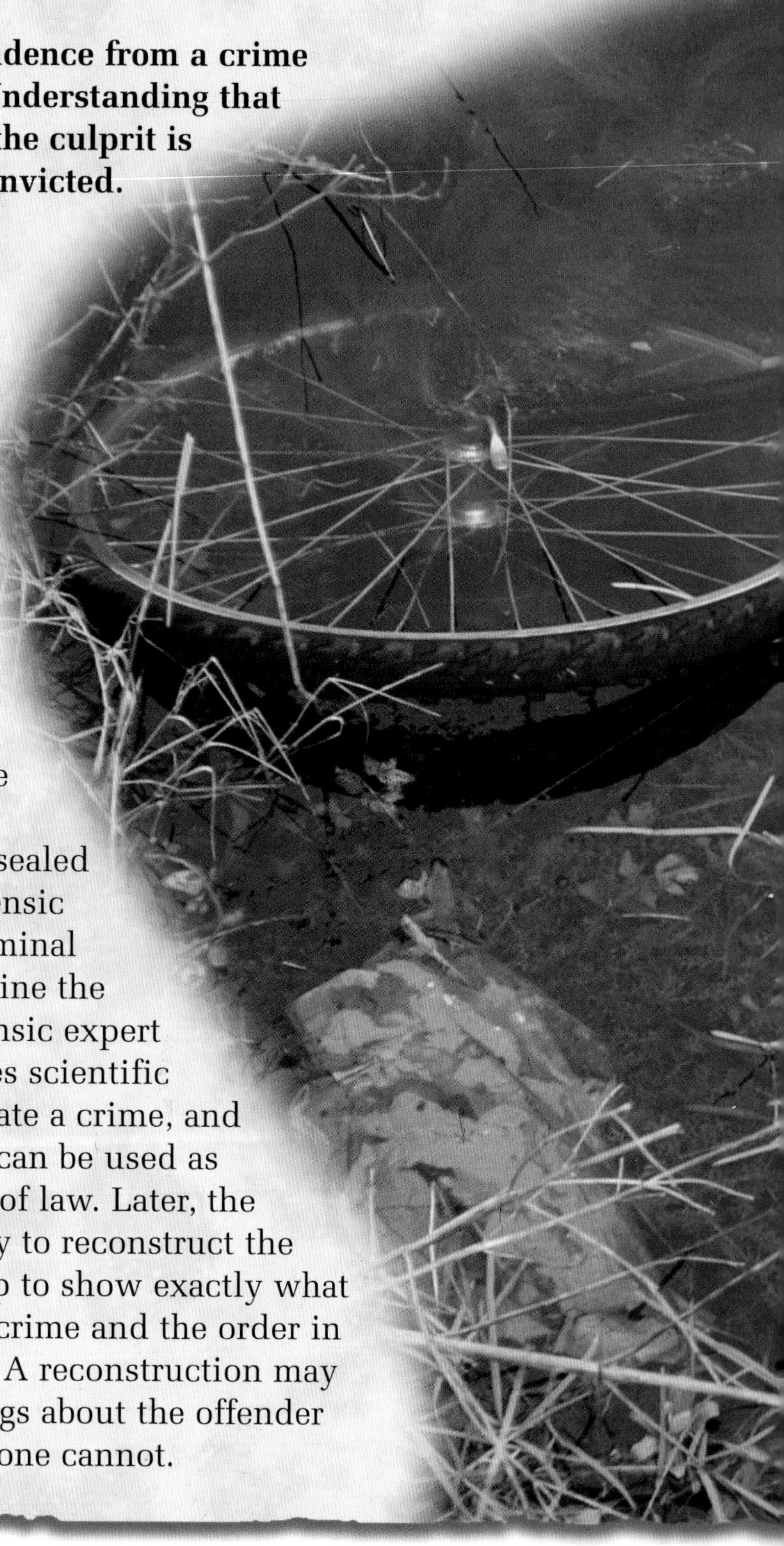

THE EVIDENCE

With any serious crime, the crime scene investigators (CSI) are quick to start their work. Once the CSIs have decided how big the crime scene is, it is cordoned off and photographed, and sketches are made. Any evidence found is recorded, photographed, and sealed in plastic bags. Forensic experts, such as criminal profilers, may examine the crime scene. A forensic expert is someone who uses scientific methods to investigate a crime, and whose conclusions can be used as evidence in a court of law. Later, the investigators will try to reconstruct the crime. This can help to show exactly what happened during a crime and the order in which it happened. A reconstruction may tell the profiler things about the offender that the evidence alone cannot.

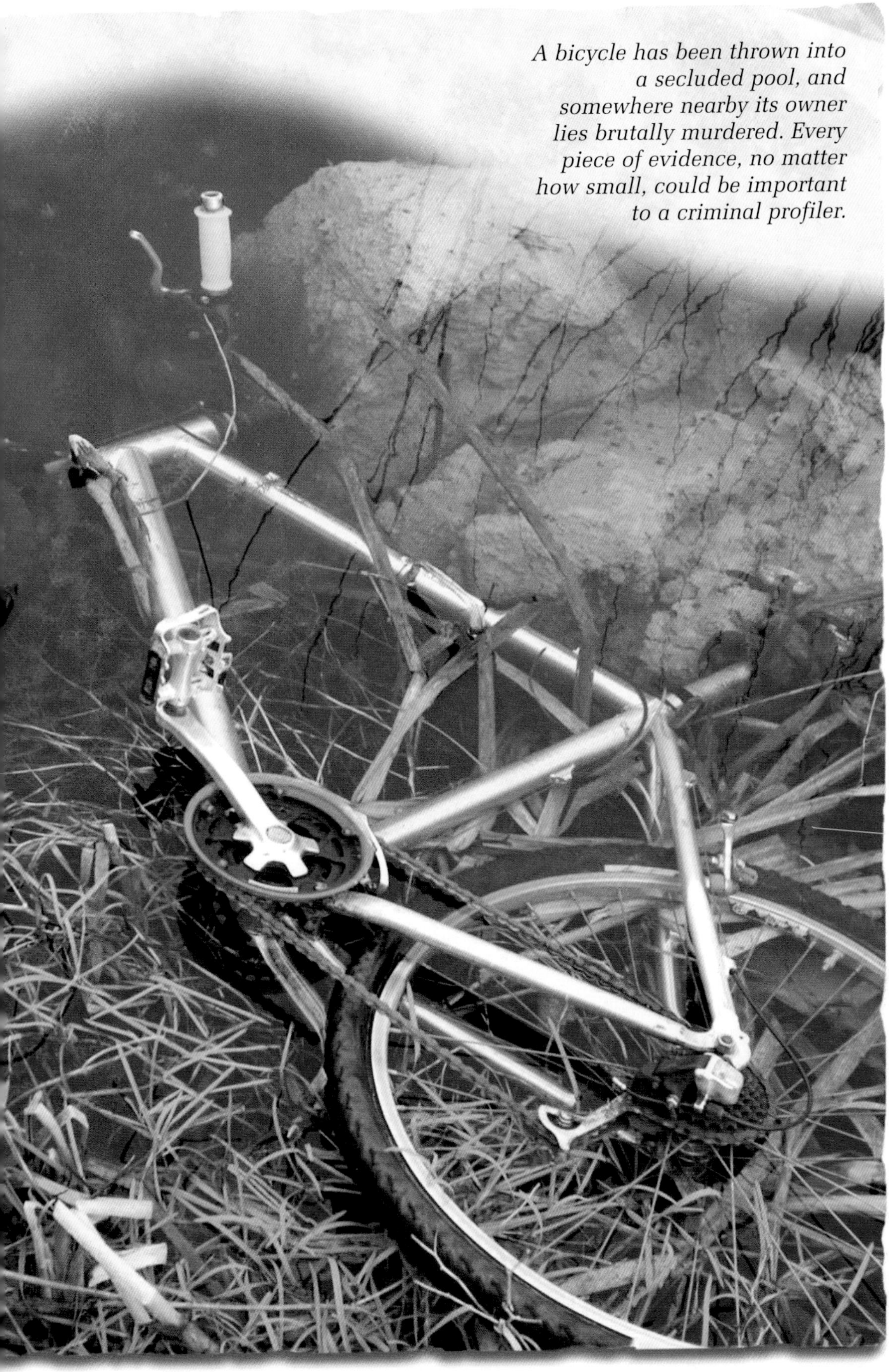

A bicycle has been thrown into a secluded pool, and somewhere nearby its owner lies brutally murdered. Every piece of evidence, no matter how small, could be important to a criminal profiler.

ALL IN THE MIND

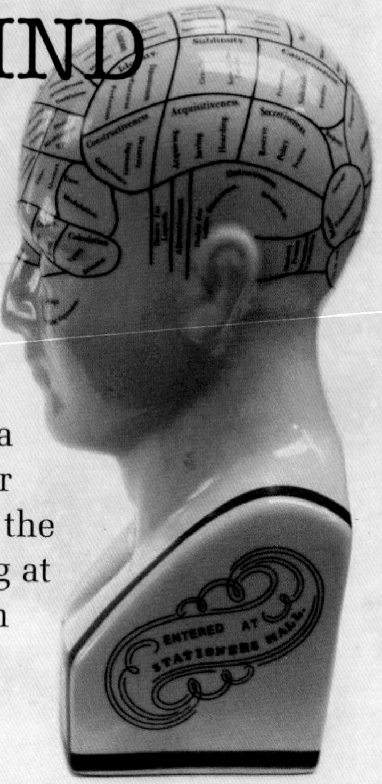
ENTERED AT STATIONERS HALL.

Some crimes are harder to solve than others, and some criminals are harder to catch. Investigators of difficult cases may ask criminal profilers for help.

Criminal Profiling

By studying the features of a crime and how a crime has been committed, a criminal profiler may be able to identify the culprit. Although the profiler rarely comes up with a name, looking at all the evidence can suggest in some detail an offender's personality and mental state. Profiling can be applied to many different types of crime, but in practice it is used mainly for crimes of violence and where the culprit is a repeat or serial criminal.

In the 1800s phrenologists believed that studying the natural bumps on people's heads could indicate if someone was a criminal or not.

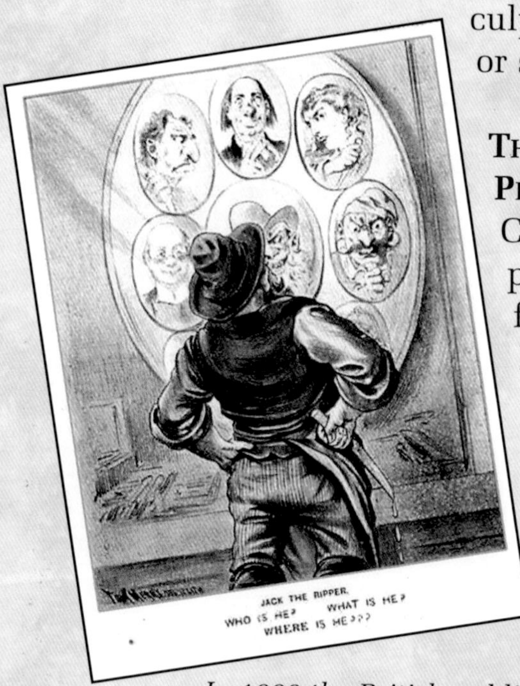
JACK THE RIPPER.
WHO IS HE? WHAT IS HE?
WHERE IS HE???

In 1888 the British public was horrified and fascinated by the crimes of "Jack the Ripper." The caption to this cartoon from an English magazine reads, "Jack the Ripper, Who is he? What is he? Where is he?"

The History of Profiling

Criminal profiling was first used in London in 1888, when Dr. Thomas Bond tried to develop a profile for the serial killer "Jack the Ripper" (see page 44). In the late nineteenth and early twentieth centuries scientists became more interested in how the mind worked. It was not until 1972 that the FBI set up its Behavioral Science Unit. This was the world's first investigative body dedicated to criminal profiling.

DEALING WITH THE EVIDENCE

A profiler will be looking for many things when examining the evidence. The method of operation, or MO, is one. This is the actions that a criminal takes to ensure that his crime is a success. Another is called the "signature." This is something criminals feel they have to do at a crime. It may be taking away a souvenir or leaving something behind. They feel that without a "signature" the crime cannot be a success. A profiler will use this evidence to discover why the crime was committed (the criminal's motive).

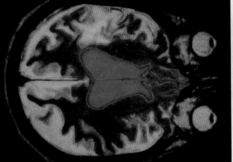

Profilers will often look at the victim. Victim profiling can shed light on the personality of the criminal.

Modern medical techniques such as MRI (Magnetic Resonance Imaging) scanning can show the connection between some criminal behavior and mental illnesses.

USING LOGIC

To understand the evidence, a profiler will use reasoning. There are two systems of reasoning or logic that the profiler may use. Inductive logic uses statistics and relies on comparing a crime to a past crime. It can assess how likely a conclusion is. Deductive logic is based on the evidence. Any theory about the crime that is not supported by the evidence is thrown out. Conclusions reached through deductive logic are final and certain.

Serial criminals nearly always look like normal people. In theory, a serial killer could be living right next door to you.

THE MAD BOMBER

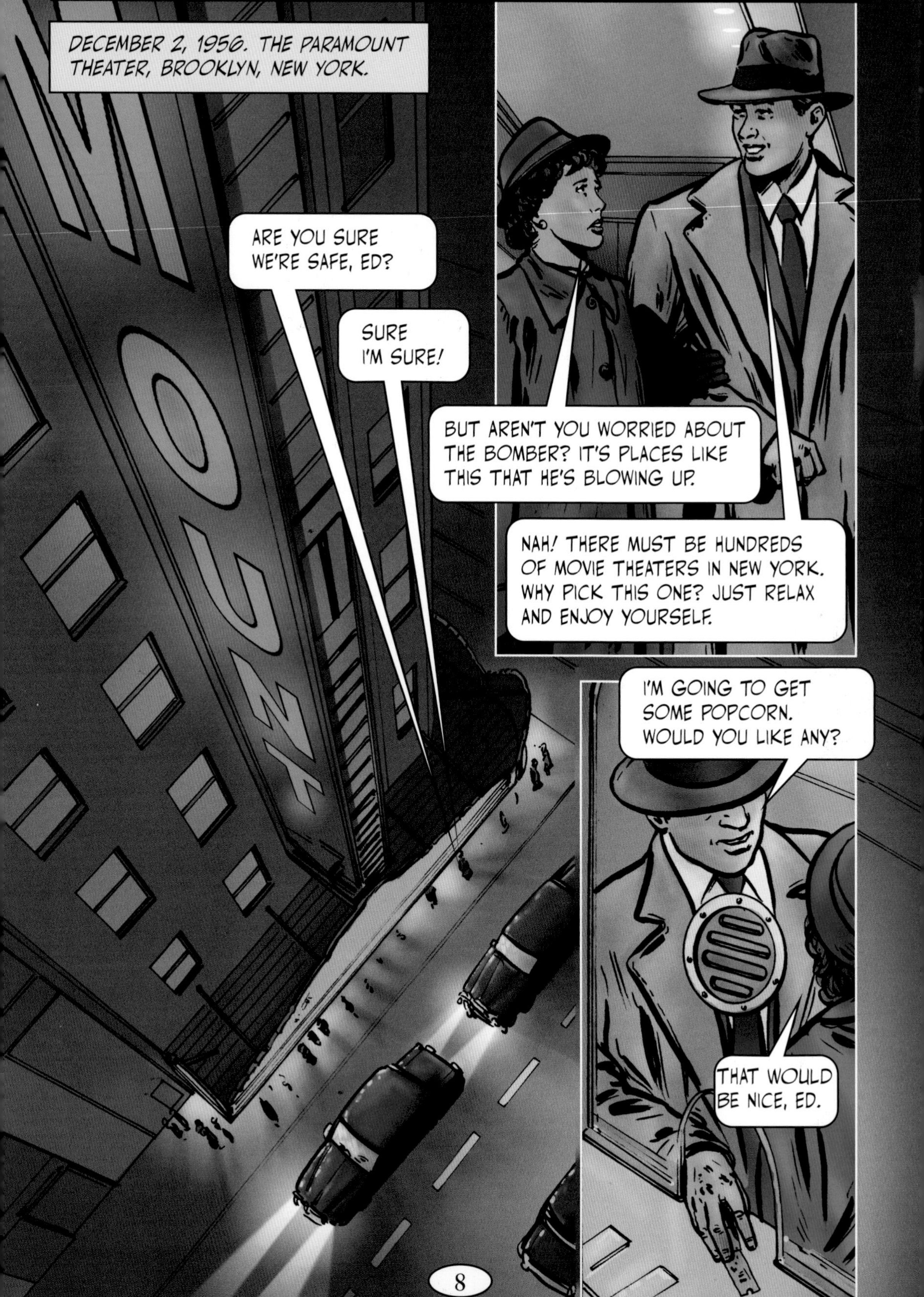
DECEMBER 2, 1956. THE PARAMOUNT THEATER, BROOKLYN, NEW YORK.
ARE YOU SURE WE'RE SAFE, ED?
SURE I'M SURE!
BUT AREN'T YOU WORRIED ABOUT THE BOMBER? IT'S PLACES LIKE THIS THAT HE'S BLOWING UP.
NAH! THERE MUST BE HUNDREDS OF MOVIE THEATERS IN NEW YORK. WHY PICK THIS ONE? JUST RELAX AND ENJOY YOURSELF.
I'M GOING TO GET SOME POPCORN. WOULD YOU LIKE ANY?
THAT WOULD BE NICE, ED.

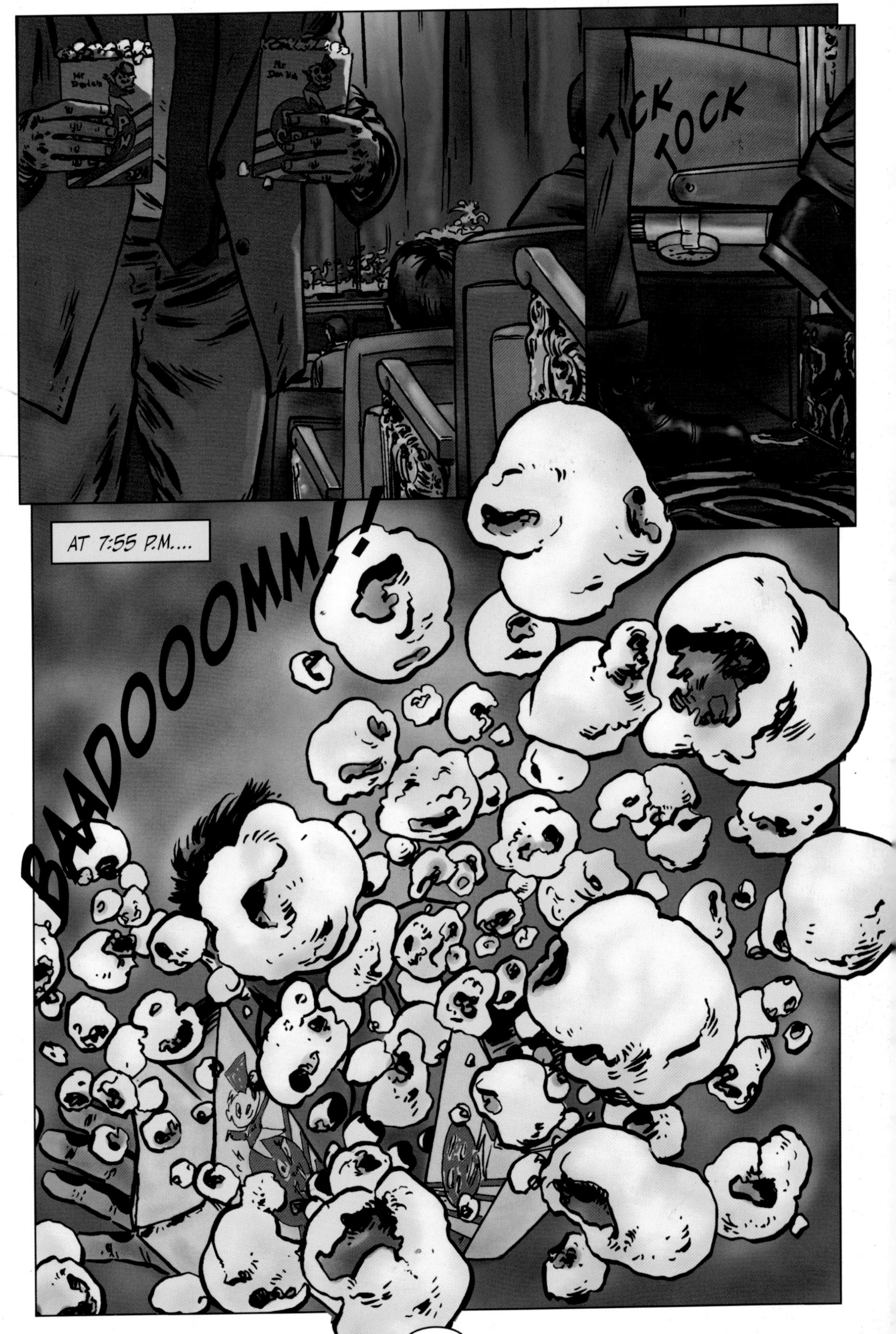
TICK TOCK
AT 7:55 P.M....
BAADOOOMM!!

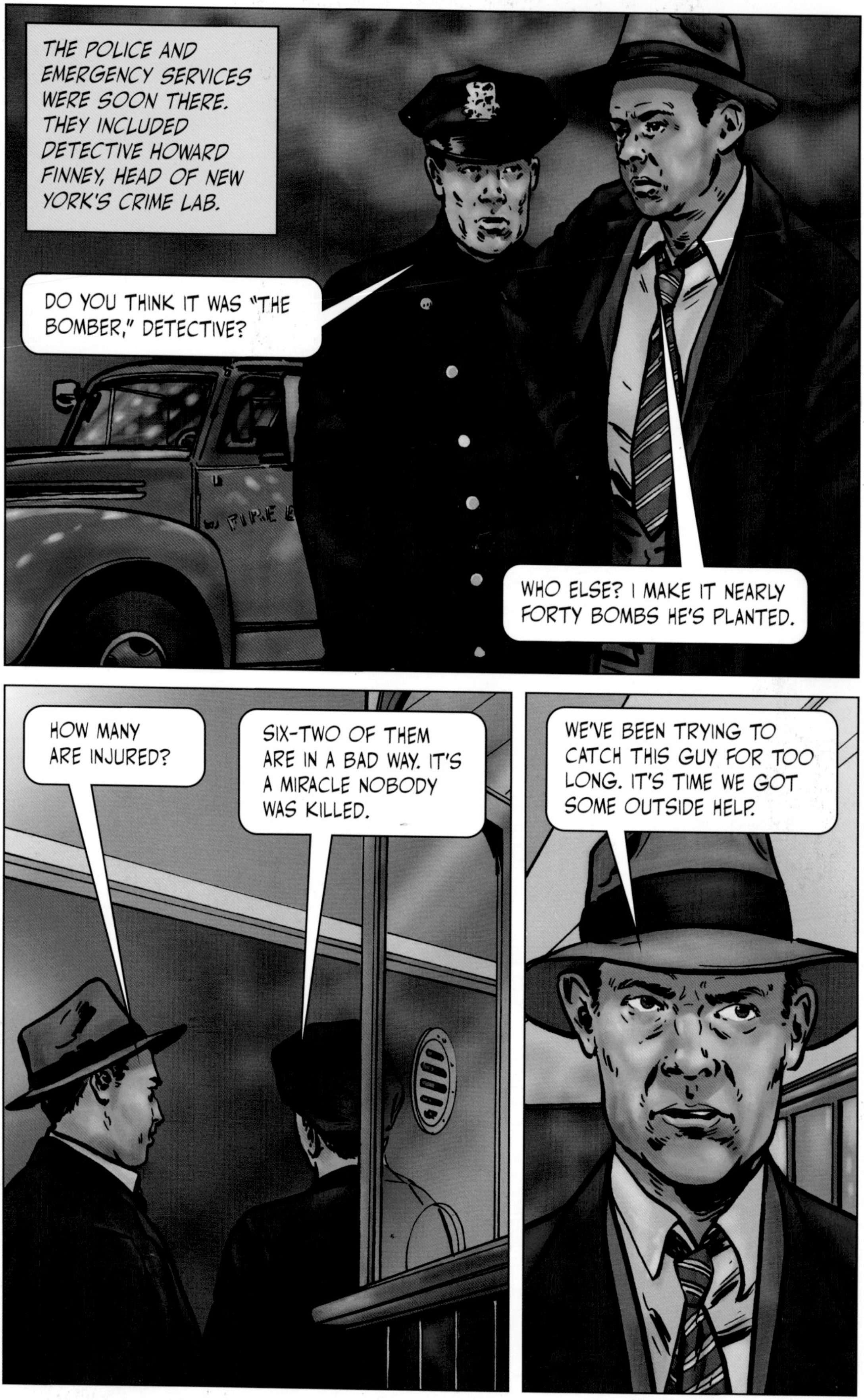
THE POLICE AND EMERGENCY SERVICES WERE SOON THERE. THEY INCLUDED DETECTIVE HOWARD FINNEY, HEAD OF NEW YORK'S CRIME LAB.
DO YOU THINK IT WAS "THE BOMBER," DETECTIVE?
WHO ELSE? I MAKE IT NEARLY FORTY BOMBS HE'S PLANTED.
HOW MANY ARE INJURED?
SIX-TWO OF THEM ARE IN A BAD WAY. IT'S A MIRACLE NOBODY WAS KILLED.
WE'VE BEEN TRYING TO CATCH THIS GUY FOR TOO LONG. IT'S TIME WE GOT SOME OUTSIDE HELP.

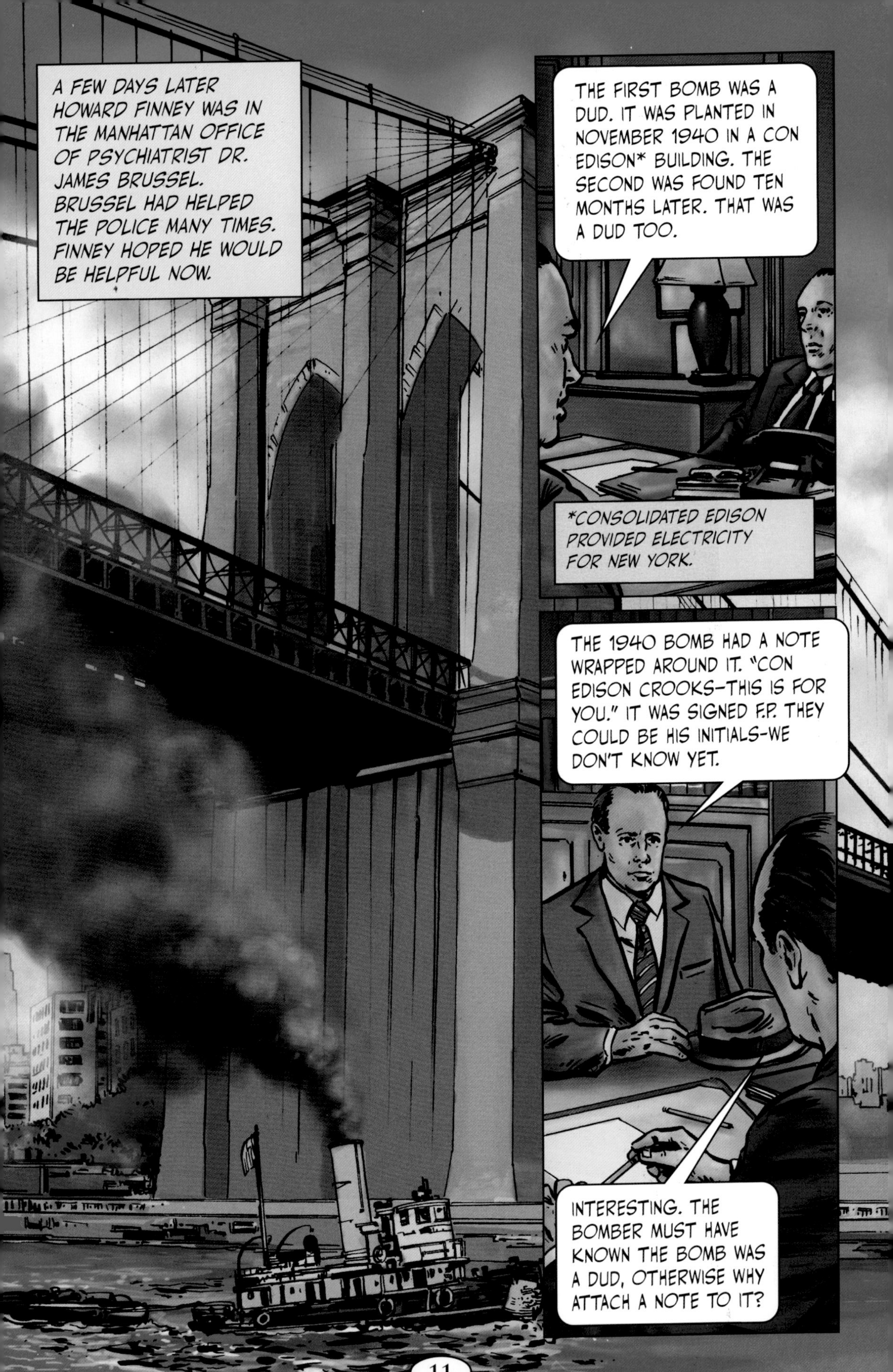
A FEW DAYS LATER HOWARD FINNEY WAS IN THE MANHATTAN OFFICE OF PSYCHIATRIST DR. JAMES BRUSSEL. BRUSSEL HAD HELPED THE POLICE MANY TIMES. FINNEY HOPED HE WOULD BE HELPFUL NOW.
THE FIRST BOMB WAS A DUD. IT WAS PLANTED IN NOVEMBER 1940 IN A CON EDISON* BUILDING. THE SECOND WAS FOUND TEN MONTHS LATER. THAT WAS A DUD TOO.
*CONSOLIDATED EDISON PROVIDED ELECTRICITY FOR NEW YORK.
THE 1940 BOMB HAD A NOTE WRAPPED AROUND IT. "CON EDISON CROOKS–THIS IS FOR YOU." IT WAS SIGNED F.P. THEY COULD BE HIS INITIALS–WE DON'T KNOW YET.
INTERESTING. THE BOMBER MUST HAVE KNOWN THE BOMB WAS A DUD, OTHERWISE WHY ATTACH A NOTE TO IT?

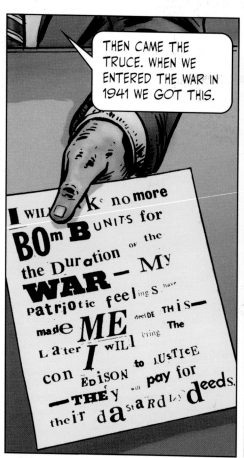

THEN CAME THE TRUCE. WHEN WE ENTERED THE WAR IN 1941 WE GOT THIS.

I WILL make no more BOmB UNITS for the Duration of the WAR—My patriotic feelings have made ME decIDE THiS— LaTer I wilL bring The con Edison to JUSTICE —THEy will pay for their daStardLy deeds.

"I WILL MAKE NO MORE BOMB UNITS FOR THE DURATION OF THE WAR—MY PATRIOTIC FEELINGS HAVE MADE ME DECIDE THIS—LATER I WILL BRING THE CON EDISON TO JUSTICE—THEY WILL PAY FOR THEIR DASTARDLY DEEDS."

HE WAS AS GOOD AS HIS WORD, THOUGH. HE STOPPED MAKING THE BOMBS—UNTIL MARCH 29, 1950...

GRAND CENTRAL STATION, NEW YORK CITY.

THE BOMB SQUAD RECOGNIZED IT RIGHT AWAY. LIKE HIS FIRST TWO, THE BOMB WAS A DUD. WE THOUGHT MAYBE HE DIDN'T MEAN FOR THEM TO GO OFF. WE SOON FOUND OUT WE WERE WRONG...

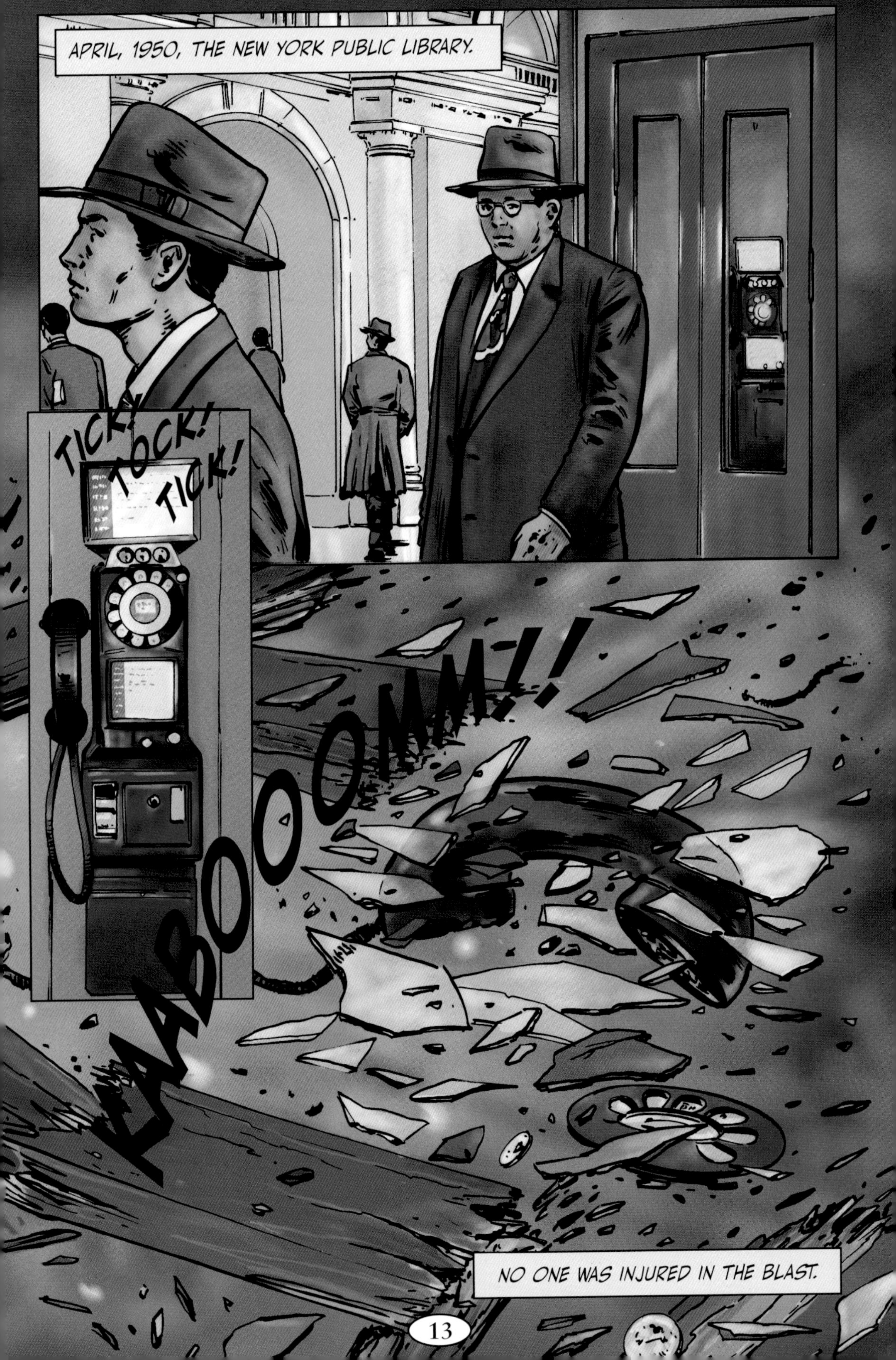
APRIL, 1950, THE NEW YORK PUBLIC LIBRARY.
TICK! TOCK! TICK!
KABOOOMM!!
NO ONE WAS INJURED IN THE BLAST.

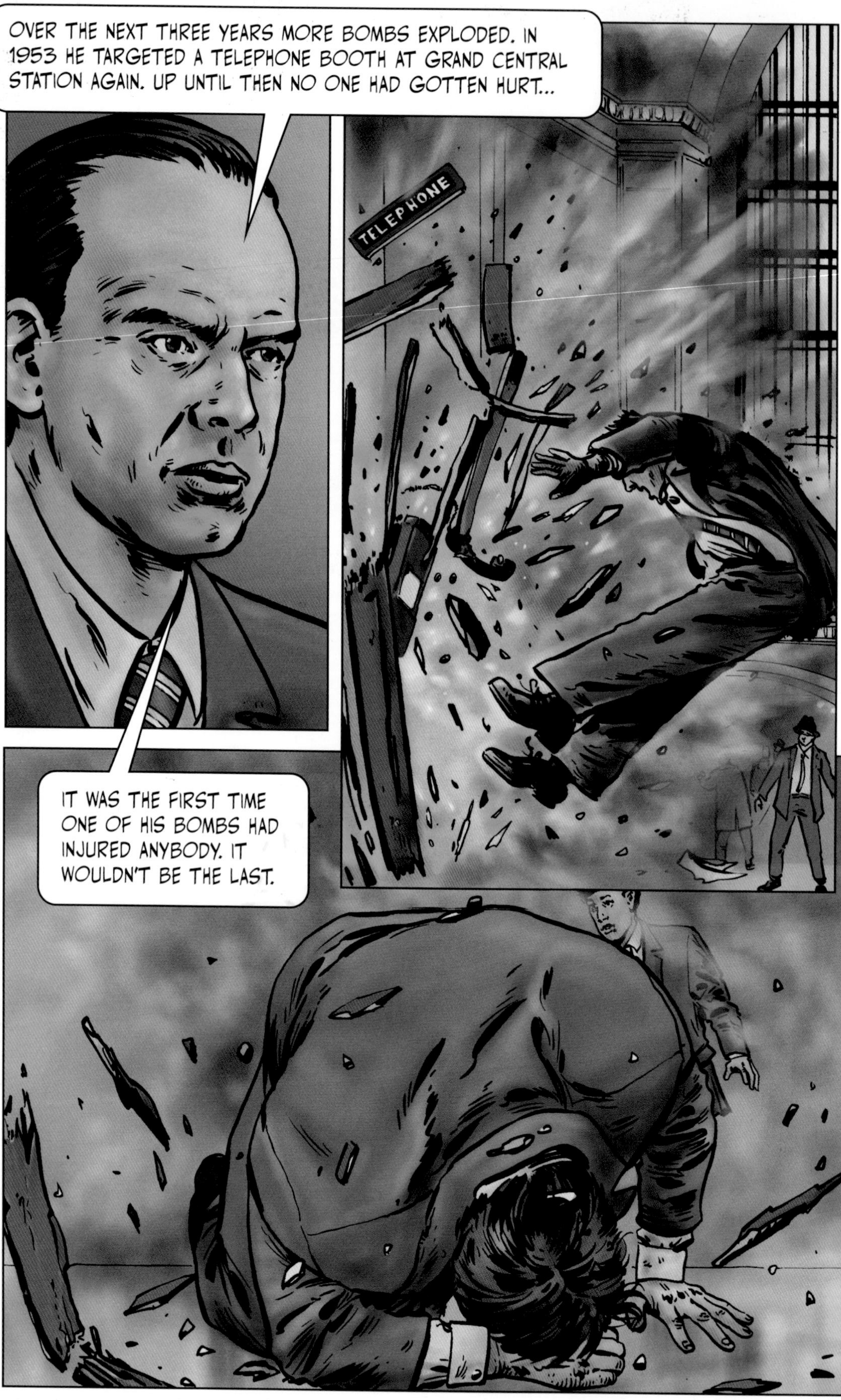
OVER THE NEXT THREE YEARS MORE BOMBS EXPLODED. IN 1953 HE TARGETED A TELEPHONE BOOTH AT GRAND CENTRAL STATION AGAIN. UP UNTIL THEN NO ONE HAD GOTTEN HURT...
TELEPHONE
IT WAS THE FIRST TIME ONE OF HIS BOMBS HAD INJURED ANYBODY. IT WOULDN'T BE THE LAST.

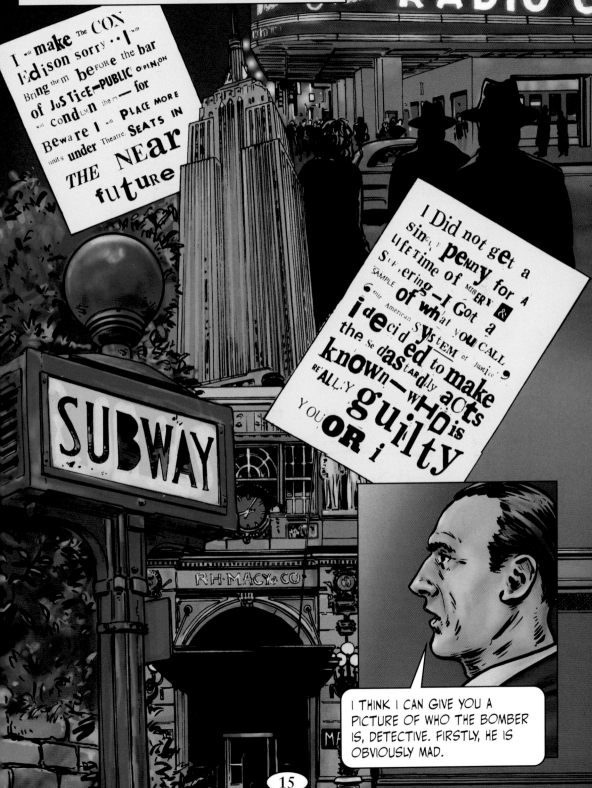

BOMBS WERE PLANTED IN PLACES THAT USED CON EDISON'S ELECTRICITY. AS WELL AS THE BOMBS, LETTERS WERE SENT TO THEATERS, RESTAURANTS, NEWSPAPERS, HOTELS, DEPARTMENT STORES—ALL THREATENING CON EDISON AND ALL OF THEM SIGNED "F.P."

I will make The CON Edison sorry... I will Bring them before the bar of JUSTICE—PUBLIC OPINION will condemn them— for Beware I will PLACE MORE units under Theatre SEATS in THE NEAR future

I Did not get a single penny for A lifetime of MISERY & SAMPLE Suffering—I Got a of what you CALL 6 our American SYSTEM of JUSTICE i decided to make the Se dastardly acts known—WHO is RE'ALL'Y guilty YOU or i

I THINK I CAN GIVE YOU A PICTURE OF WHO THE BOMBER IS, DETECTIVE. FIRSTLY, HE IS OBVIOUSLY MAD.

15

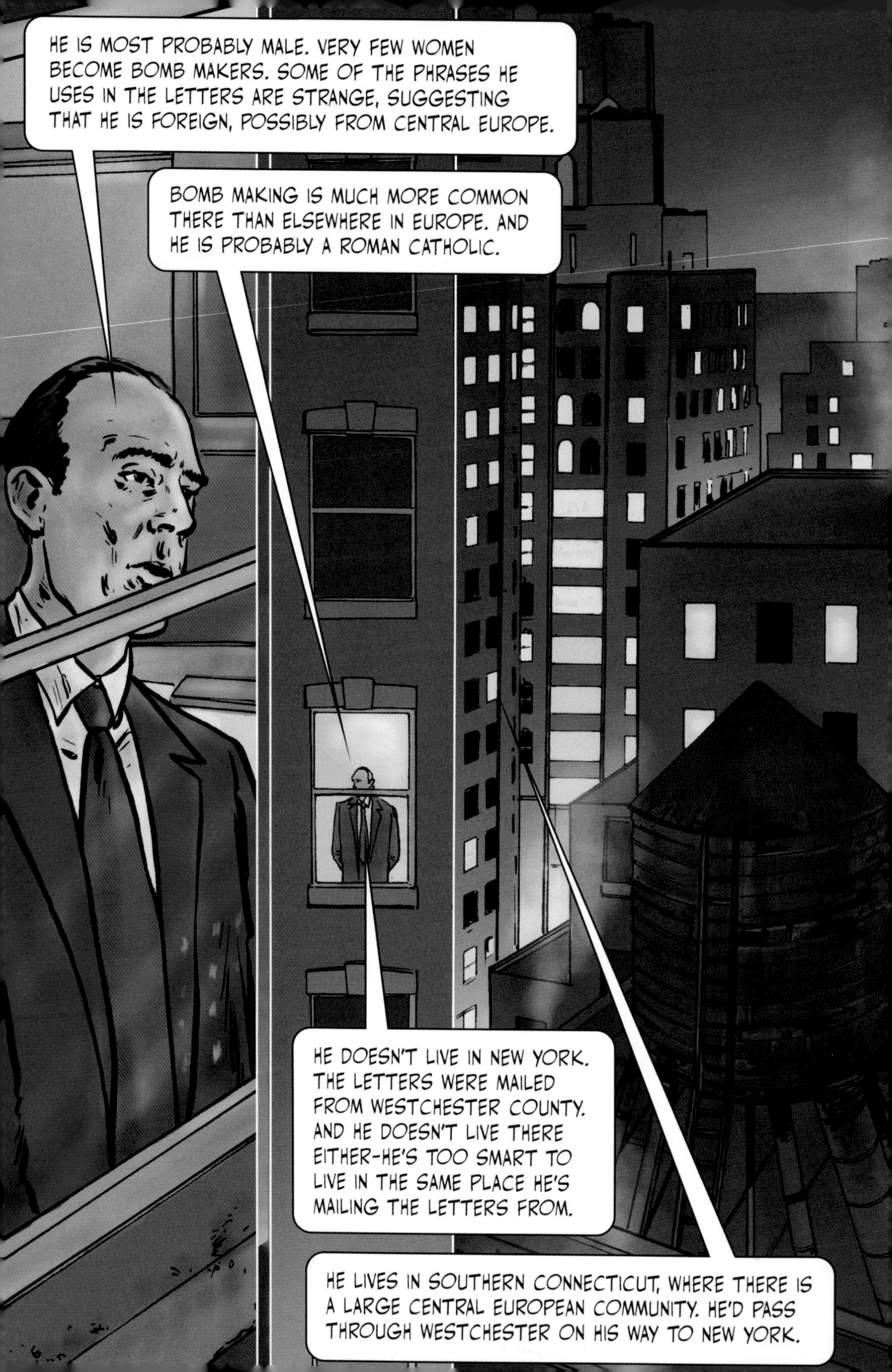
HE IS MOST PROBABLY MALE. VERY FEW WOMEN BECOME BOMB MAKERS. SOME OF THE PHRASES HE USES IN THE LETTERS ARE STRANGE, SUGGESTING THAT HE IS FOREIGN, POSSIBLY FROM CENTRAL EUROPE.
BOMB MAKING IS MUCH MORE COMMON THERE THAN ELSEWHERE IN EUROPE. AND HE IS PROBABLY A ROMAN CATHOLIC.
HE DOESN'T LIVE IN NEW YORK. THE LETTERS WERE MAILED FROM WESTCHESTER COUNTY. AND HE DOESN'T LIVE THERE EITHER—HE'S TOO SMART TO LIVE IN THE SAME PLACE HE'S MAILING THE LETTERS FROM.
HE LIVES IN SOUTHERN CONNECTICUT, WHERE THERE IS A LARGE CENTRAL EUROPEAN COMMUNITY. HE'D PASS THROUGH WESTCHESTER ON HIS WAY TO NEW YORK.

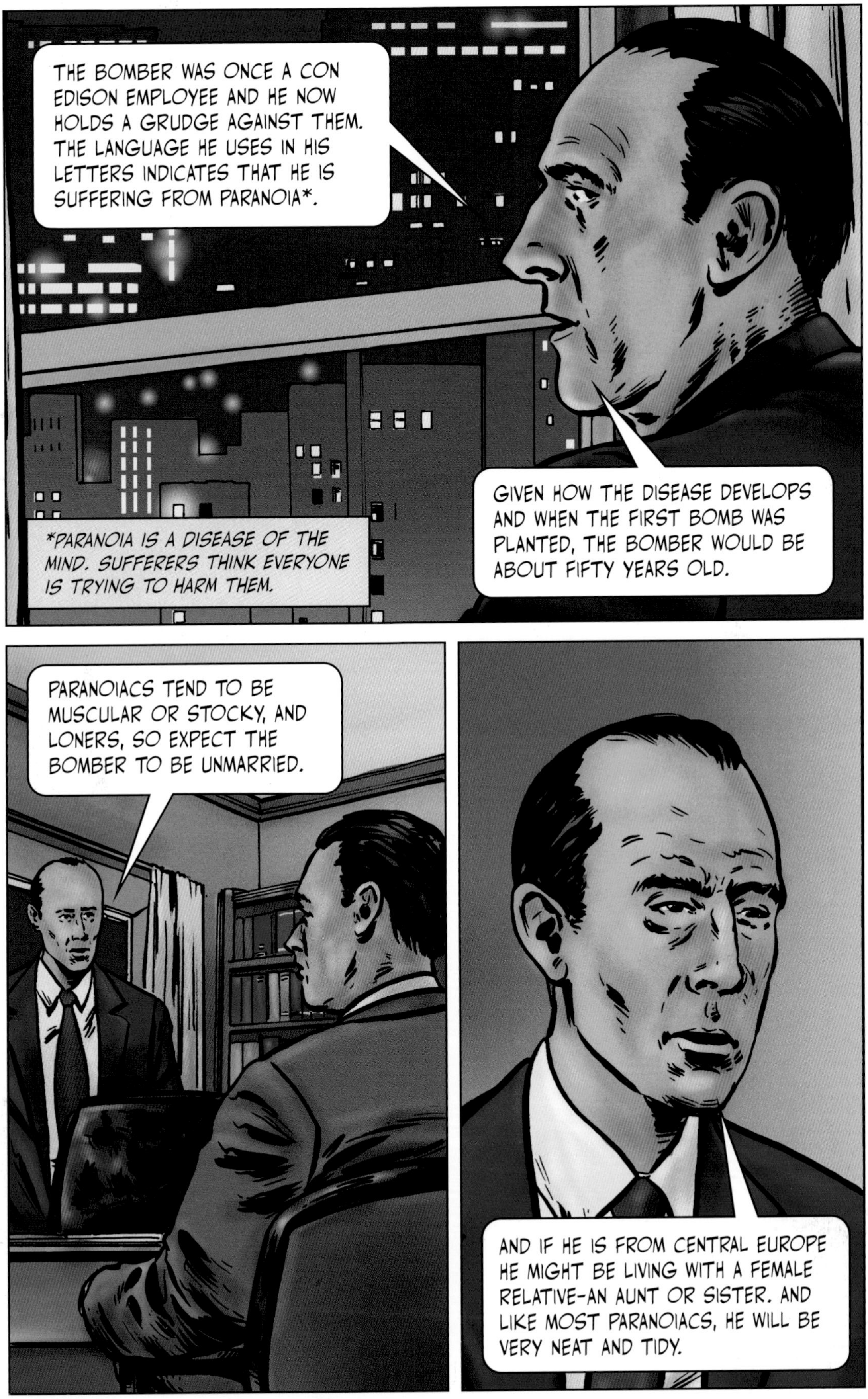
THE BOMBER WAS ONCE A CON EDISON EMPLOYEE AND HE NOW HOLDS A GRUDGE AGAINST THEM. THE LANGUAGE HE USES IN HIS LETTERS INDICATES THAT HE IS SUFFERING FROM PARANOIA*.
*PARANOIA IS A DISEASE OF THE MIND. SUFFERERS THINK EVERYONE IS TRYING TO HARM THEM.
GIVEN HOW THE DISEASE DEVELOPS AND WHEN THE FIRST BOMB WAS PLANTED, THE BOMBER WOULD BE ABOUT FIFTY YEARS OLD.
PARANOIACS TEND TO BE MUSCULAR OR STOCKY, AND LONERS, SO EXPECT THE BOMBER TO BE UNMARRIED.
AND IF HE IS FROM CENTRAL EUROPE HE MIGHT BE LIVING WITH A FEMALE RELATIVE-AN AUNT OR SISTER. AND LIKE MOST PARANOIACS, HE WILL BE VERY NEAT AND TIDY.

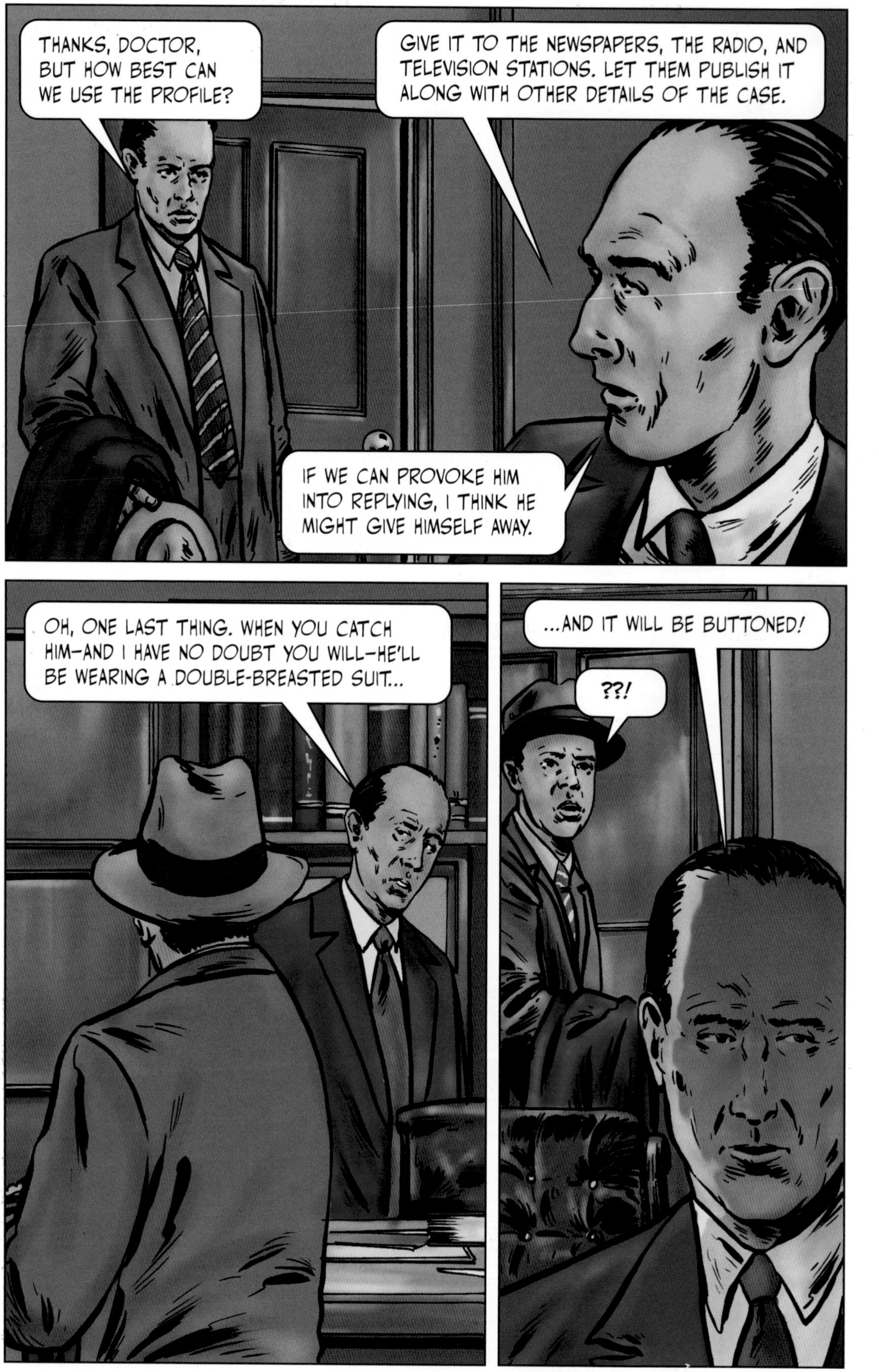
THANKS, DOCTOR, BUT HOW BEST CAN WE USE THE PROFILE?
GIVE IT TO THE NEWSPAPERS, THE RADIO, AND TELEVISION STATIONS. LET THEM PUBLISH IT ALONG WITH OTHER DETAILS OF THE CASE.
IF WE CAN PROVOKE HIM INTO REPLYING, I THINK HE MIGHT GIVE HIMSELF AWAY.
OH, ONE LAST THING. WHEN YOU CATCH HIM—AND I HAVE NO DOUBT YOU WILL—HE'LL BE WEARING A DOUBLE-BREASTED SUIT...
...AND IT WILL BE BUTTONED!
??!

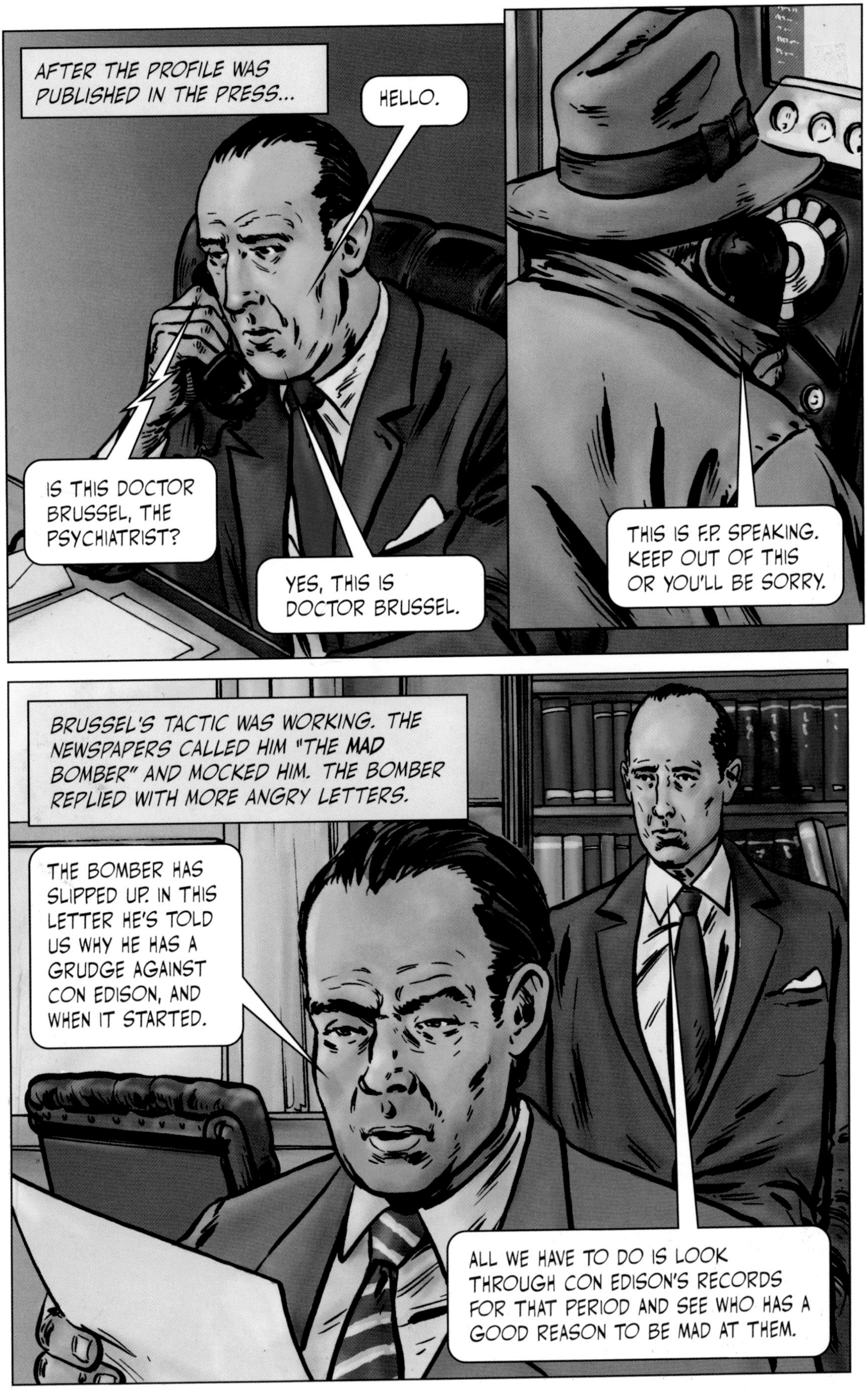
AFTER THE PROFILE WAS PUBLISHED IN THE PRESS...
HELLO.
IS THIS DOCTOR BRUSSEL, THE PSYCHIATRIST?
YES, THIS IS DOCTOR BRUSSEL.
THIS IS F.P. SPEAKING. KEEP OUT OF THIS OR YOU'LL BE SORRY.
BRUSSEL'S TACTIC WAS WORKING. THE NEWSPAPERS CALLED HIM "THE MAD BOMBER" AND MOCKED HIM. THE BOMBER REPLIED WITH MORE ANGRY LETTERS.
THE BOMBER HAS SLIPPED UP. IN THIS LETTER HE'S TOLD US WHY HE HAS A GRUDGE AGAINST CON EDISON, AND WHEN IT STARTED.
ALL WE HAVE TO DO IS LOOK THROUGH CON EDISON'S RECORDS FOR THAT PERIOD AND SEE WHO HAS A GOOD REASON TO BE MAD AT THEM.

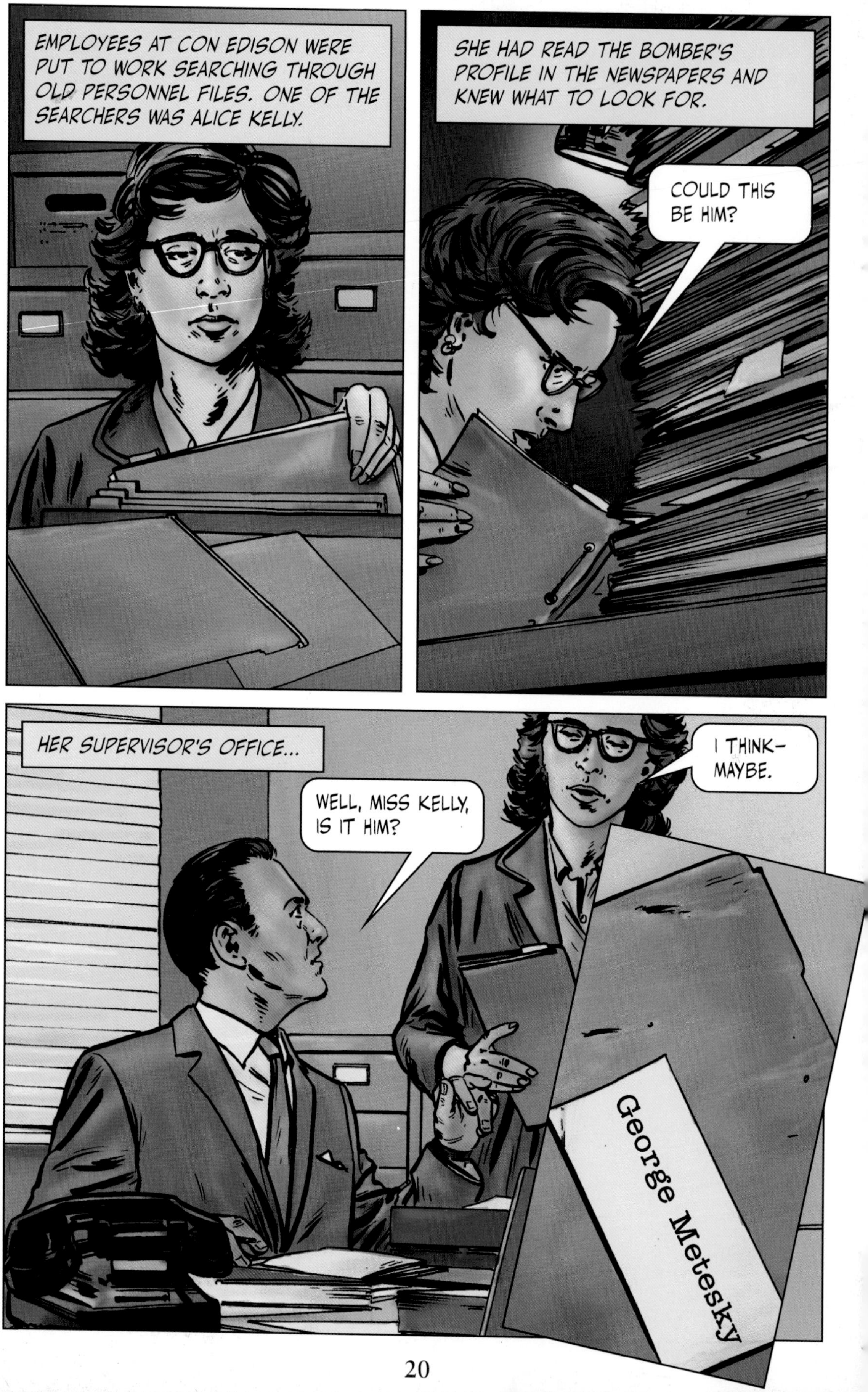
EMPLOYEES AT CON EDISON WERE PUT TO WORK SEARCHING THROUGH OLD PERSONNEL FILES. ONE OF THE SEARCHERS WAS ALICE KELLY.
SHE HAD READ THE BOMBER'S PROFILE IN THE NEWSPAPERS AND KNEW WHAT TO LOOK FOR.
COULD THIS BE HIM?
HER SUPERVISOR'S OFFICE...
WELL, MISS KELLY, IS IT HIM?
I THINK- MAYBE.
George Metesky

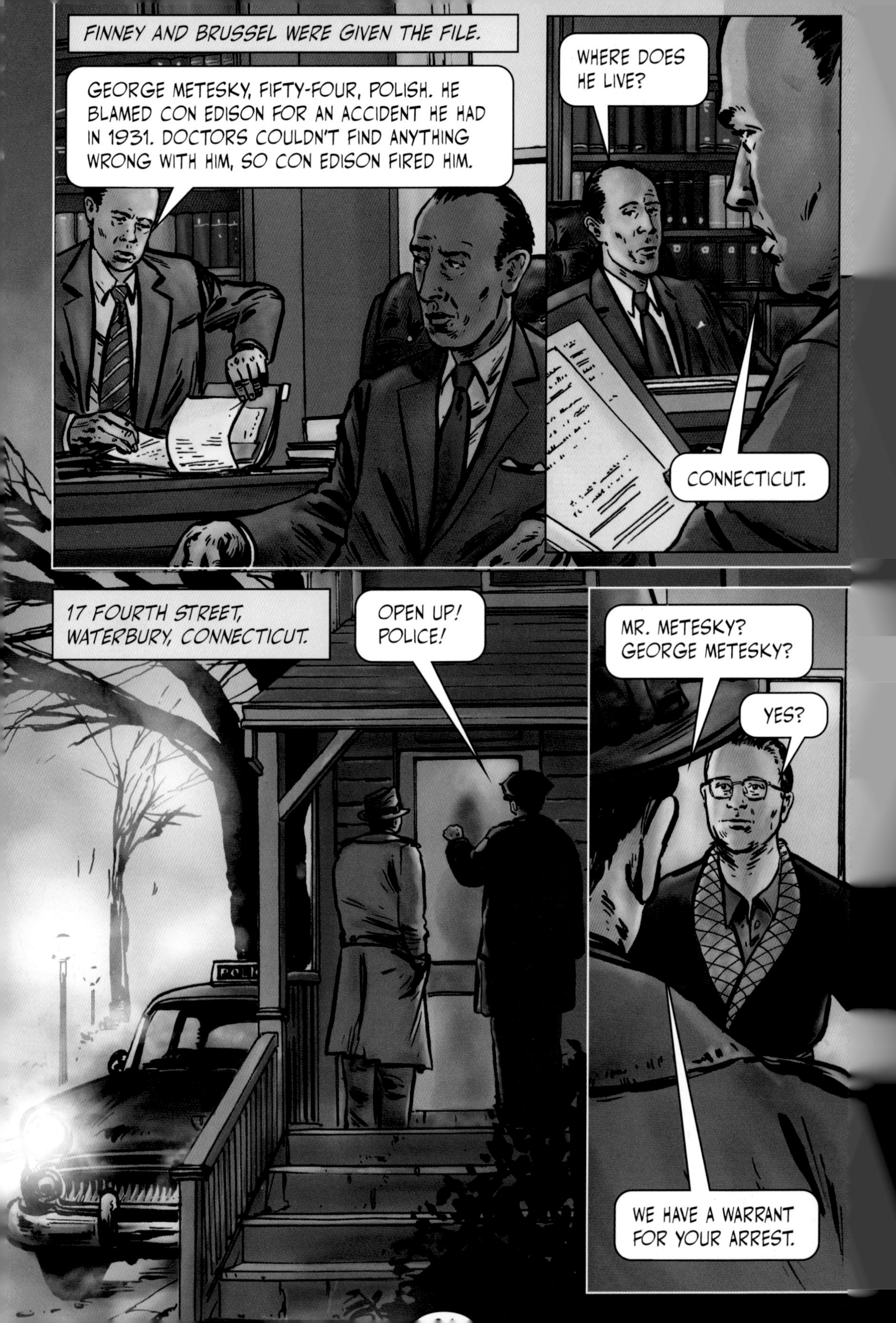
FINNEY AND BRUSSEL WERE GIVEN THE FILE.
GEORGE METESKY, FIFTY-FOUR, POLISH. HE BLAMED CON EDISON FOR AN ACCIDENT HE HAD IN 1931. DOCTORS COULDN'T FIND ANYTHING WRONG WITH HIM, SO CON EDISON FIRED HIM.
WHERE DOES HE LIVE?
CONNECTICUT.
17 FOURTH STREET, WATERBURY, CONNECTICUT.
OPEN UP! POLICE!
MR. METESKY? GEORGE METESKY?
YES?
WE HAVE A WARRANT FOR YOUR ARREST.

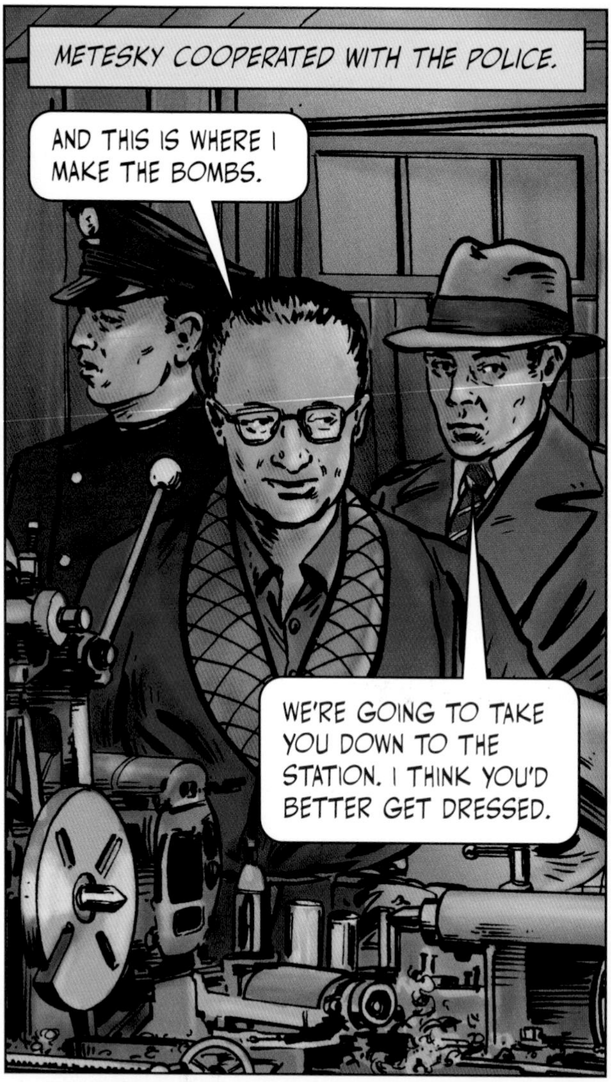
METESKY COOPERATED WITH THE POLICE.
AND THIS IS WHERE I MAKE THE BOMBS.
WE'RE GOING TO TAKE YOU DOWN TO THE STATION. I THINK YOU'D BETTER GET DRESSED.

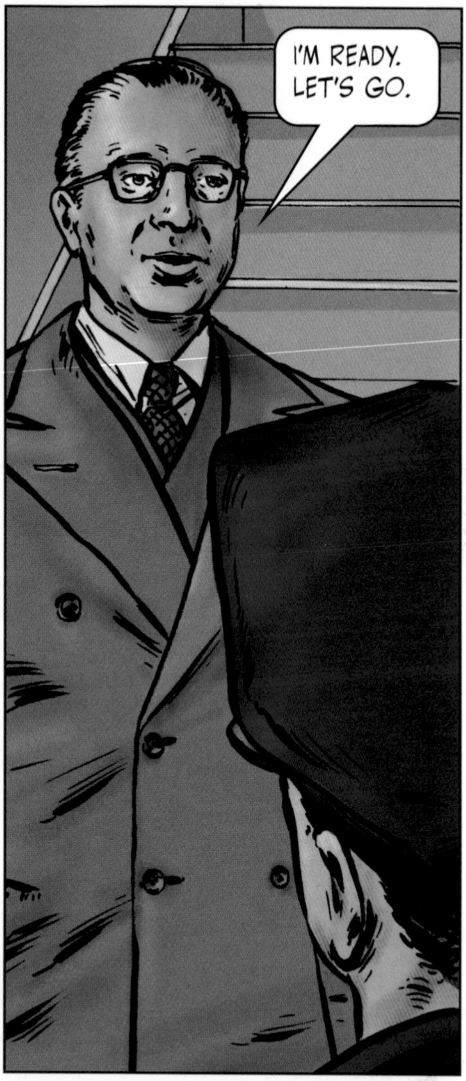
I'M READY. LET'S GO.

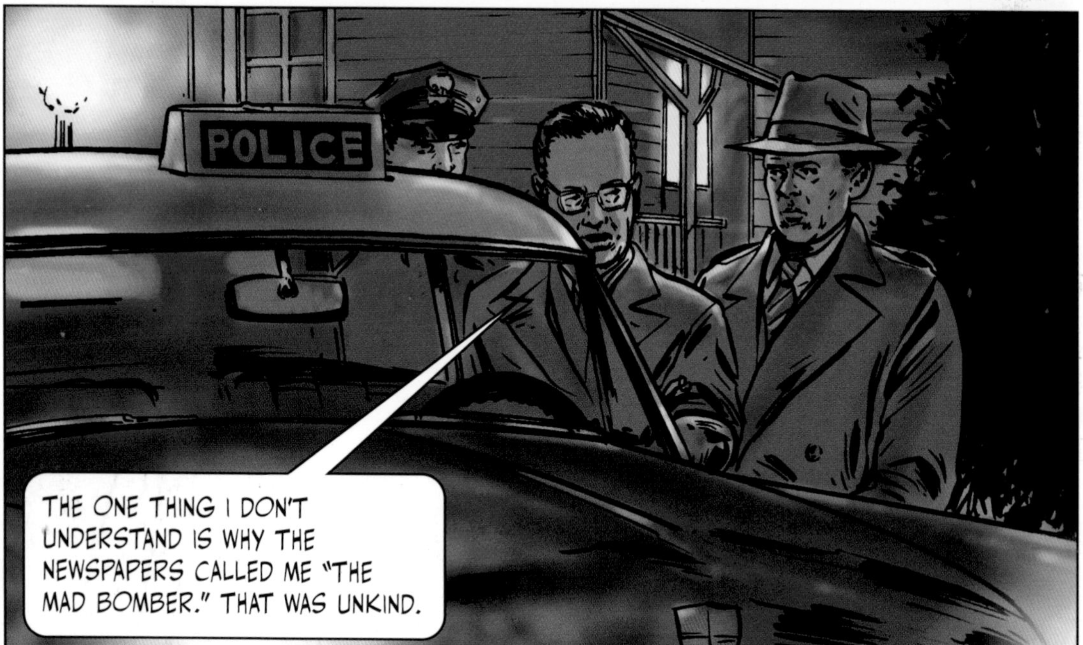
POLICE
THE ONE THING I DON'T UNDERSTAND IS WHY THE NEWSPAPERS CALLED ME "THE MAD BOMBER." THAT WAS UNKIND.

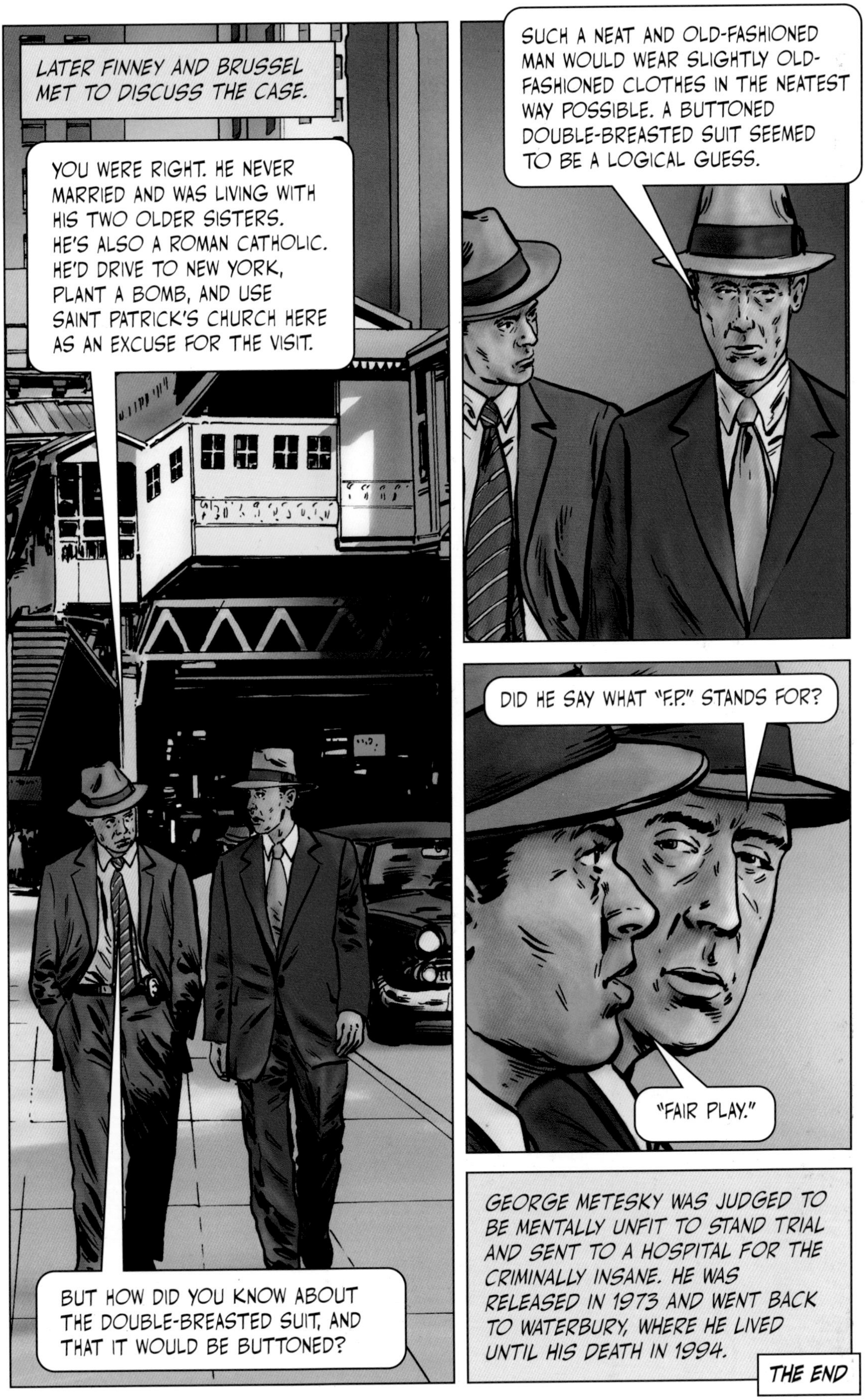
LATER FINNEY AND BRUSSEL MET TO DISCUSS THE CASE.
YOU WERE RIGHT. HE NEVER MARRIED AND WAS LIVING WITH HIS TWO OLDER SISTERS. HE'S ALSO A ROMAN CATHOLIC. HE'D DRIVE TO NEW YORK, PLANT A BOMB, AND USE SAINT PATRICK'S CHURCH HERE AS AN EXCUSE FOR THE VISIT.
BUT HOW DID YOU KNOW ABOUT THE DOUBLE-BREASTED SUIT, AND THAT IT WOULD BE BUTTONED?
SUCH A NEAT AND OLD-FASHIONED MAN WOULD WEAR SLIGHTLY OLD-FASHIONED CLOTHES IN THE NEATEST WAY POSSIBLE. A BUTTONED DOUBLE-BREASTED SUIT SEEMED TO BE A LOGICAL GUESS.
DID HE SAY WHAT "F.P." STANDS FOR?
"FAIR PLAY."
GEORGE METESKY WAS JUDGED TO BE MENTALLY UNFIT TO STAND TRIAL AND SENT TO A HOSPITAL FOR THE CRIMINALLY INSANE. HE WAS RELEASED IN 1973 AND WENT BACK TO WATERBURY, WHERE HE LIVED UNTIL HIS DEATH IN 1994.
THE END

THE TYLENOL MURDERS

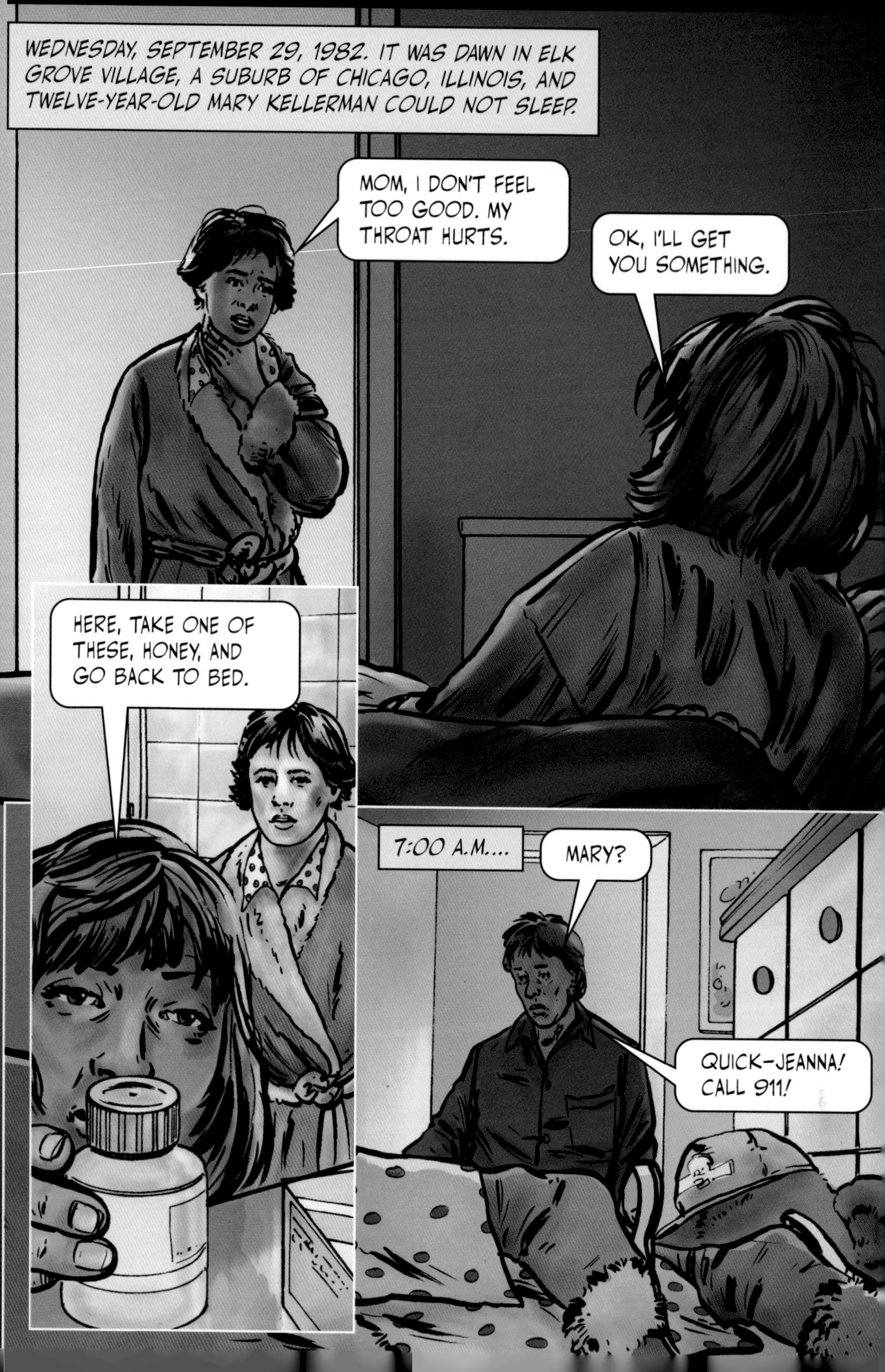
WEDNESDAY, SEPTEMBER 29, 1982. IT WAS DAWN IN ELK GROVE VILLAGE, A SUBURB OF CHICAGO, ILLINOIS, AND TWELVE-YEAR-OLD MARY KELLERMAN COULD NOT SLEEP.
MOM, I DON'T FEEL TOO GOOD. MY THROAT HURTS.
OK, I'LL GET YOU SOMETHING.
HERE, TAKE ONE OF THESE, HONEY, AND GO BACK TO BED.
7:00 A.M....
MARY?
QUICK–JEANNA! CALL 911!

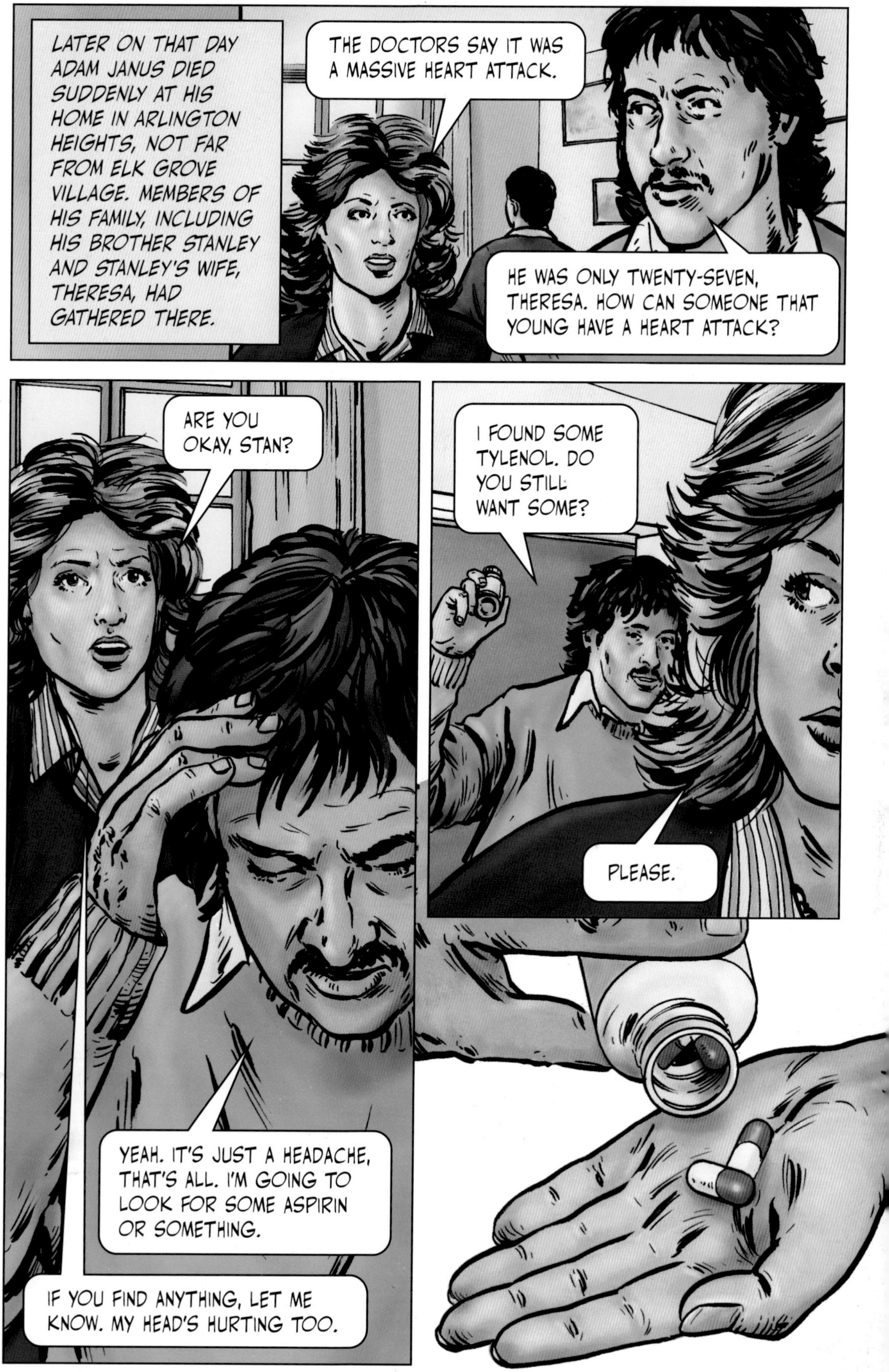
LATER ON THAT DAY ADAM JANUS DIED SUDDENLY AT HIS HOME IN ARLINGTON HEIGHTS, NOT FAR FROM ELK GROVE VILLAGE. MEMBERS OF HIS FAMILY, INCLUDING HIS BROTHER STANLEY AND STANLEY'S WIFE, THERESA, HAD GATHERED THERE.
THE DOCTORS SAY IT WAS A MASSIVE HEART ATTACK.
HE WAS ONLY TWENTY-SEVEN, THERESA. HOW CAN SOMEONE THAT YOUNG HAVE A HEART ATTACK?
ARE YOU OKAY, STAN?
YEAH. IT'S JUST A HEADACHE, THAT'S ALL. I'M GOING TO LOOK FOR SOME ASPIRIN OR SOMETHING.
IF YOU FIND ANYTHING, LET ME KNOW. MY HEAD'S HURTING TOO.
I FOUND SOME TYLENOL. DO YOU STILL WANT SOME?
PLEASE.

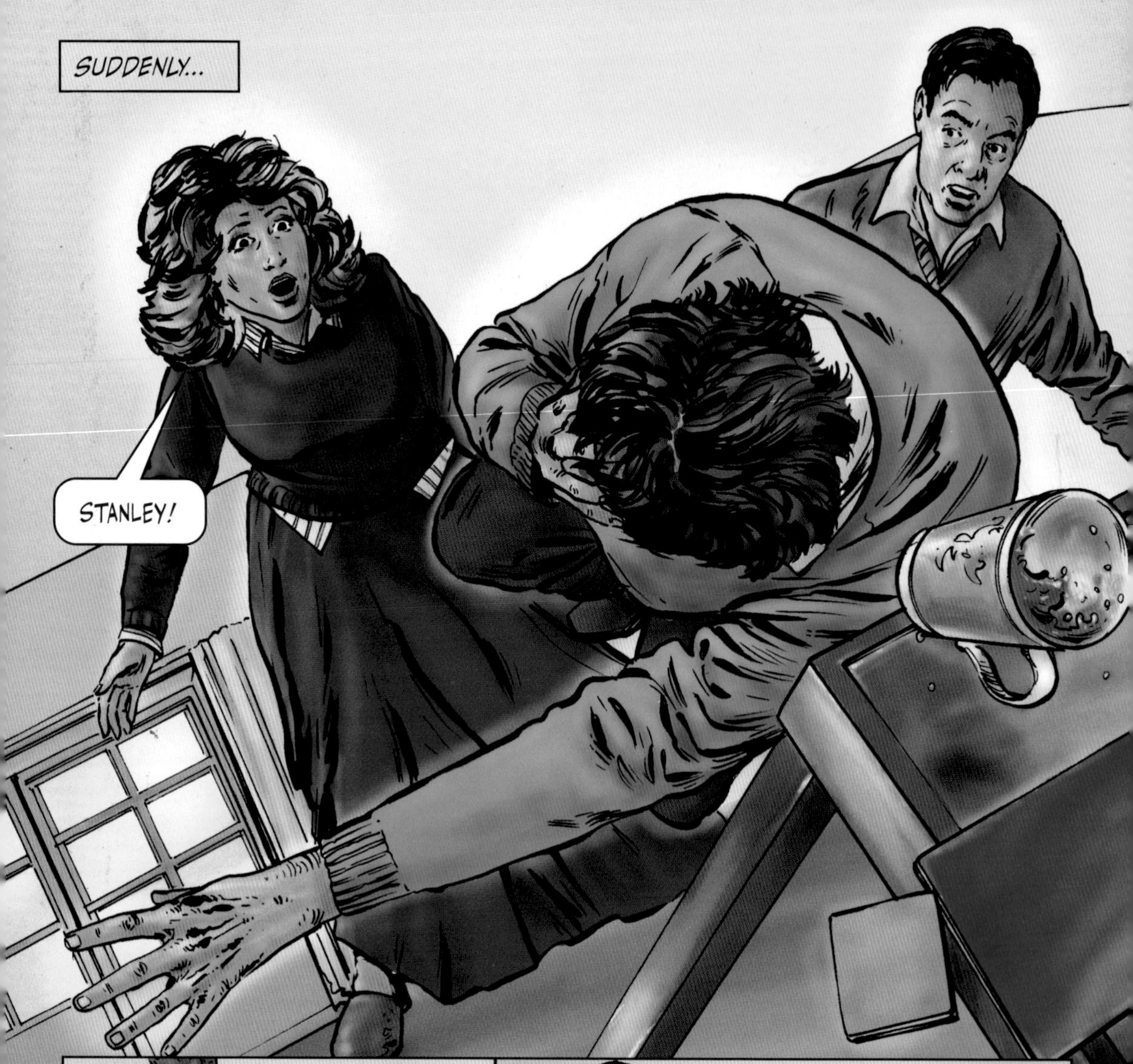
SUDDENLY...
STANLEY!

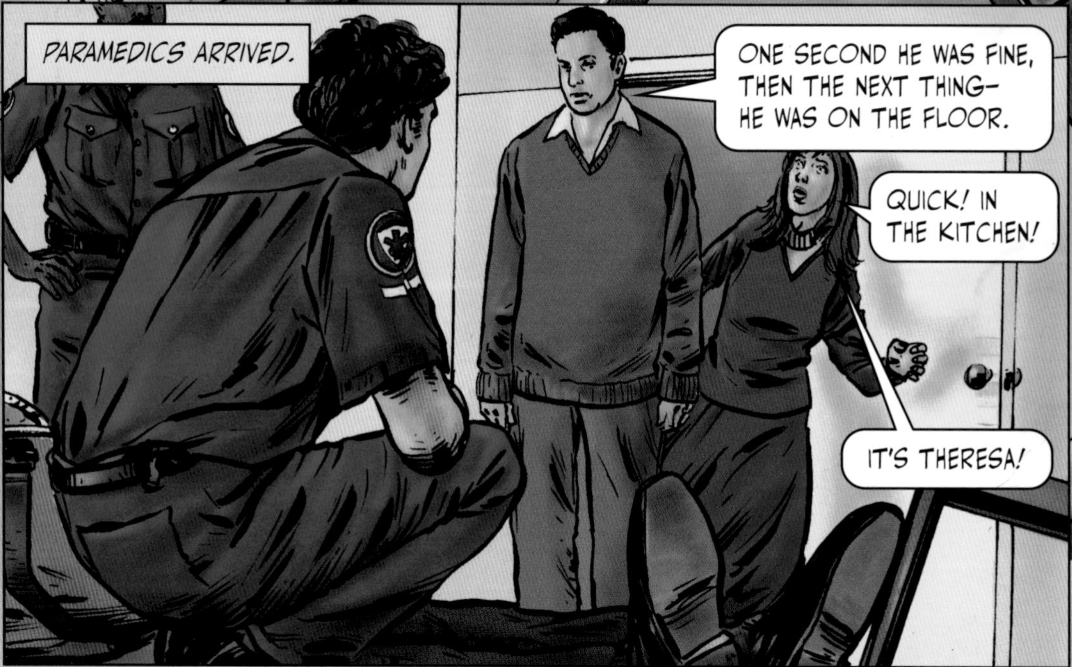
PARAMEDICS ARRIVED.
ONE SECOND HE WAS FINE, THEN THE NEXT THING– HE WAS ON THE FLOOR.
QUICK! IN THE KITCHEN!
IT'S THERESA!

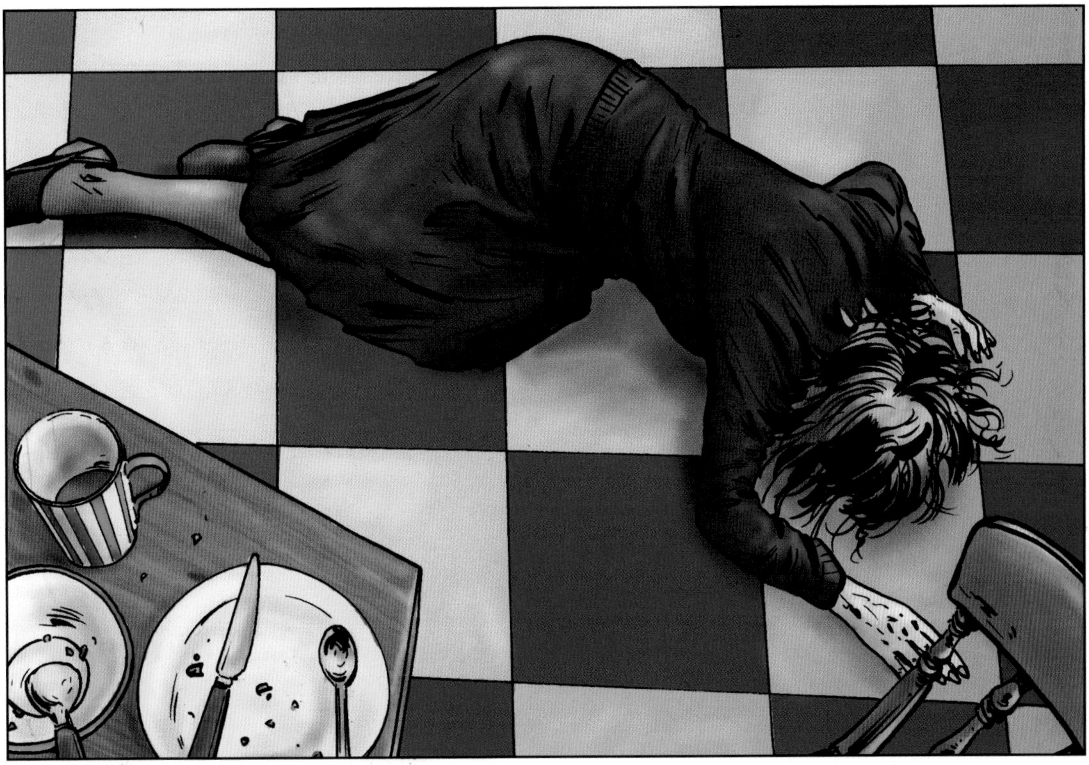

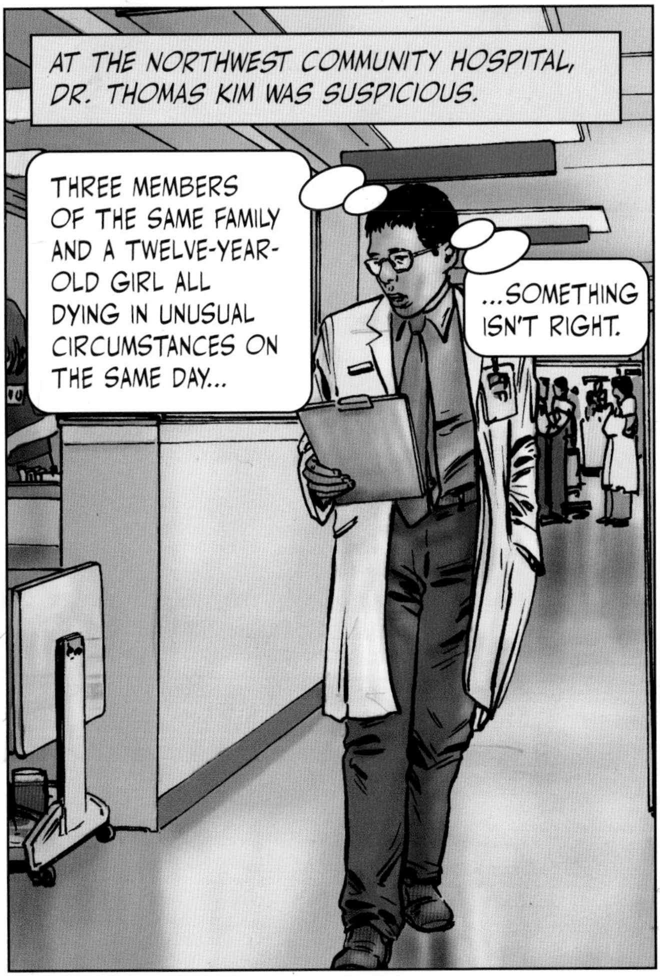
AT THE NORTHWEST COMMUNITY HOSPITAL, DR. THOMAS KIM WAS SUSPICIOUS.
THREE MEMBERS OF THE SAME FAMILY AND A TWELVE-YEAR-OLD GIRL ALL DYING IN UNUSUAL CIRCUMSTANCES ON THE SAME DAY...
...SOMETHING ISN'T RIGHT.

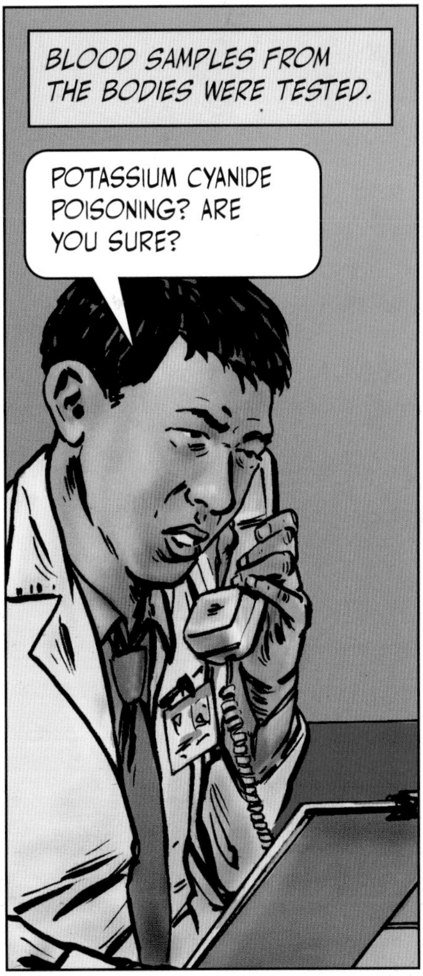
BLOOD SAMPLES FROM THE BODIES WERE TESTED.
POTASSIUM CYANIDE POISONING? ARE YOU SURE?

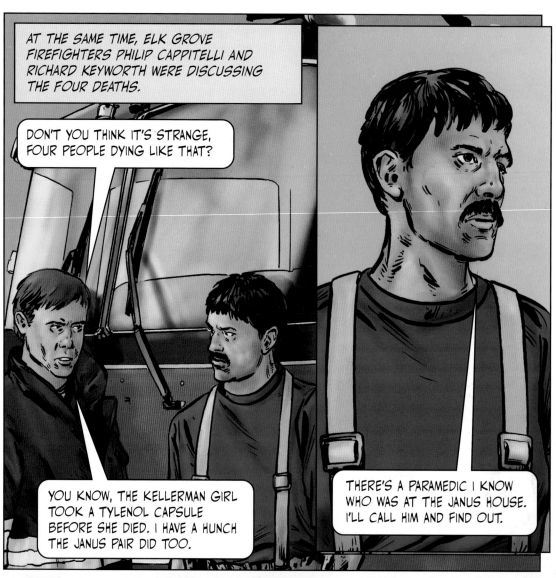

AT THE SAME TIME, ELK GROVE FIREFIGHTERS PHILIP CAPPITELLI AND RICHARD KEYWORTH WERE DISCUSSING THE FOUR DEATHS.

DON'T YOU THINK IT'S STRANGE, FOUR PEOPLE DYING LIKE THAT?

YOU KNOW, THE KELLERMAN GIRL TOOK A TYLENOL CAPSULE BEFORE SHE DIED. I HAVE A HUNCH THE JANUS PAIR DID TOO.

THERE'S A PARAMEDIC I KNOW WHO WAS AT THE JANUS HOUSE. I'LL CALL HIM AND FIND OUT.

YOUR HUNCH WAS RIGHT, PHIL, THE JANUS COUPLE DID TAKE TYLENOL CAPSULES BEFORE THEY DIED. I THINK WE SHOULD CALL THE POLICE.

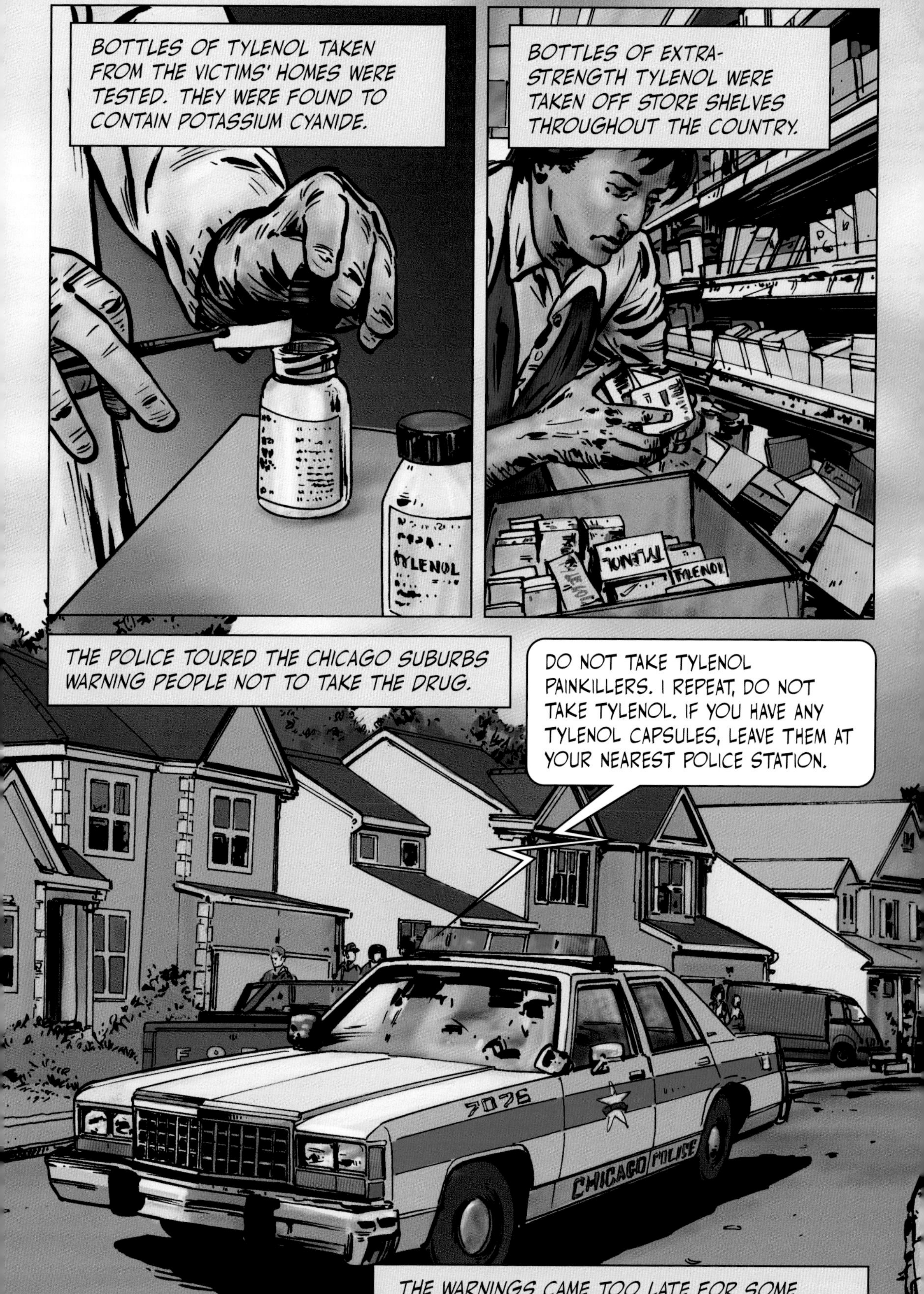
BOTTLES OF TYLENOL TAKEN FROM THE VICTIMS' HOMES WERE TESTED. THEY WERE FOUND TO CONTAIN POTASSIUM CYANIDE.
TYLENOL
BOTTLES OF EXTRA-STRENGTH TYLENOL WERE TAKEN OFF STORE SHELVES THROUGHOUT THE COUNTRY.
TYLENOL
THE POLICE TOURED THE CHICAGO SUBURBS WARNING PEOPLE NOT TO TAKE THE DRUG.
DO NOT TAKE TYLENOL PAINKILLERS. I REPEAT, DO NOT TAKE TYLENOL. IF YOU HAVE ANY TYLENOL CAPSULES, LEAVE THEM AT YOUR NEAREST POLICE STATION.
7076
CHICAGO POLICE
THE WARNINGS CAME TOO LATE FOR SOME. BY FRIDAY THREE MORE PEOPLE HAD DIED.

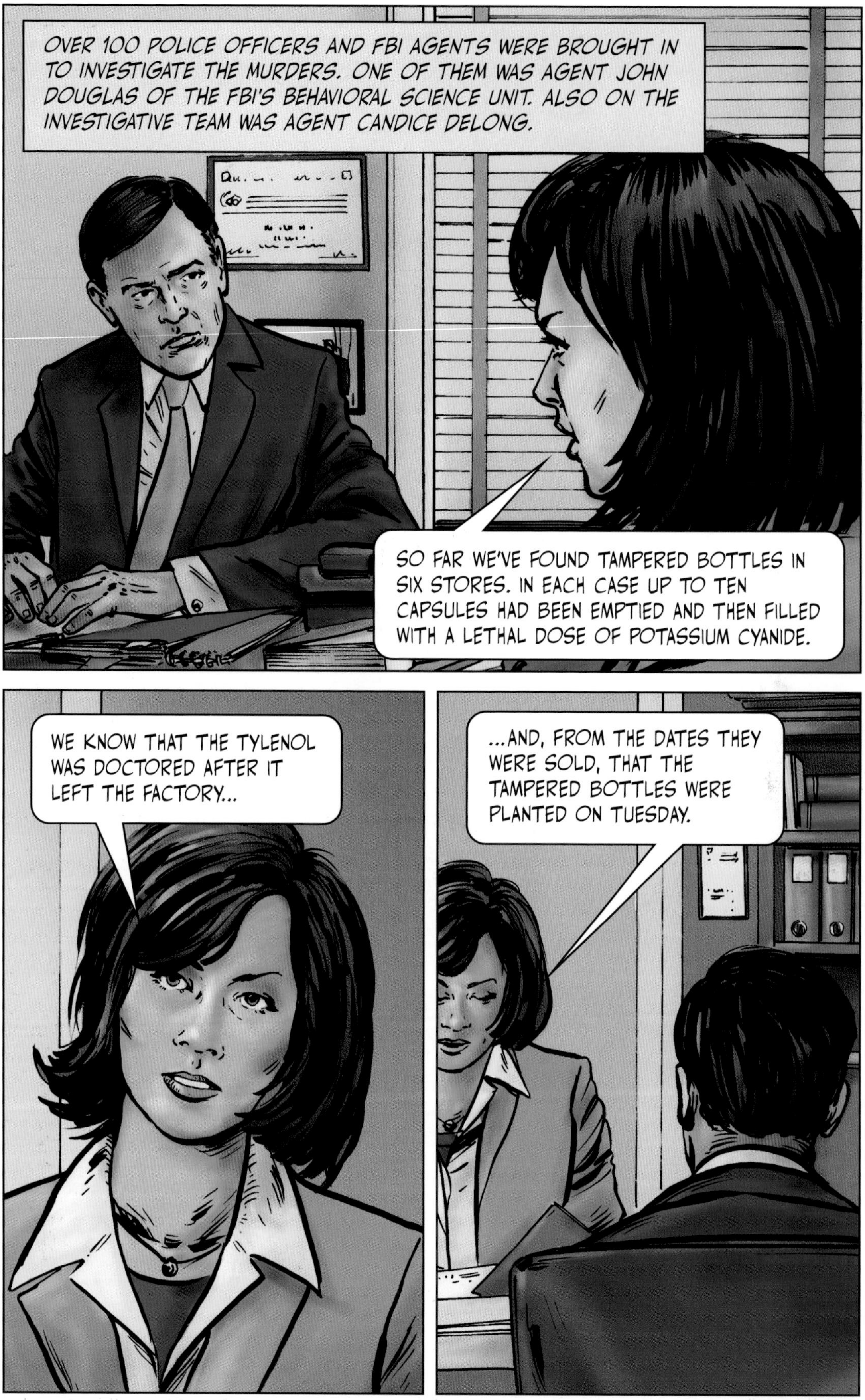
OVER 100 POLICE OFFICERS AND FBI AGENTS WERE BROUGHT IN TO INVESTIGATE THE MURDERS. ONE OF THEM WAS AGENT JOHN DOUGLAS OF THE FBI'S BEHAVIORAL SCIENCE UNIT. ALSO ON THE INVESTIGATIVE TEAM WAS AGENT CANDICE DELONG.
SO FAR WE'VE FOUND TAMPERED BOTTLES IN SIX STORES. IN EACH CASE UP TO TEN CAPSULES HAD BEEN EMPTIED AND THEN FILLED WITH A LETHAL DOSE OF POTASSIUM CYANIDE.
WE KNOW THAT THE TYLENOL WAS DOCTORED AFTER IT LEFT THE FACTORY...
...AND, FROM THE DATES THEY WERE SOLD, THAT THE TAMPERED BOTTLES WERE PLANTED ON TUESDAY.

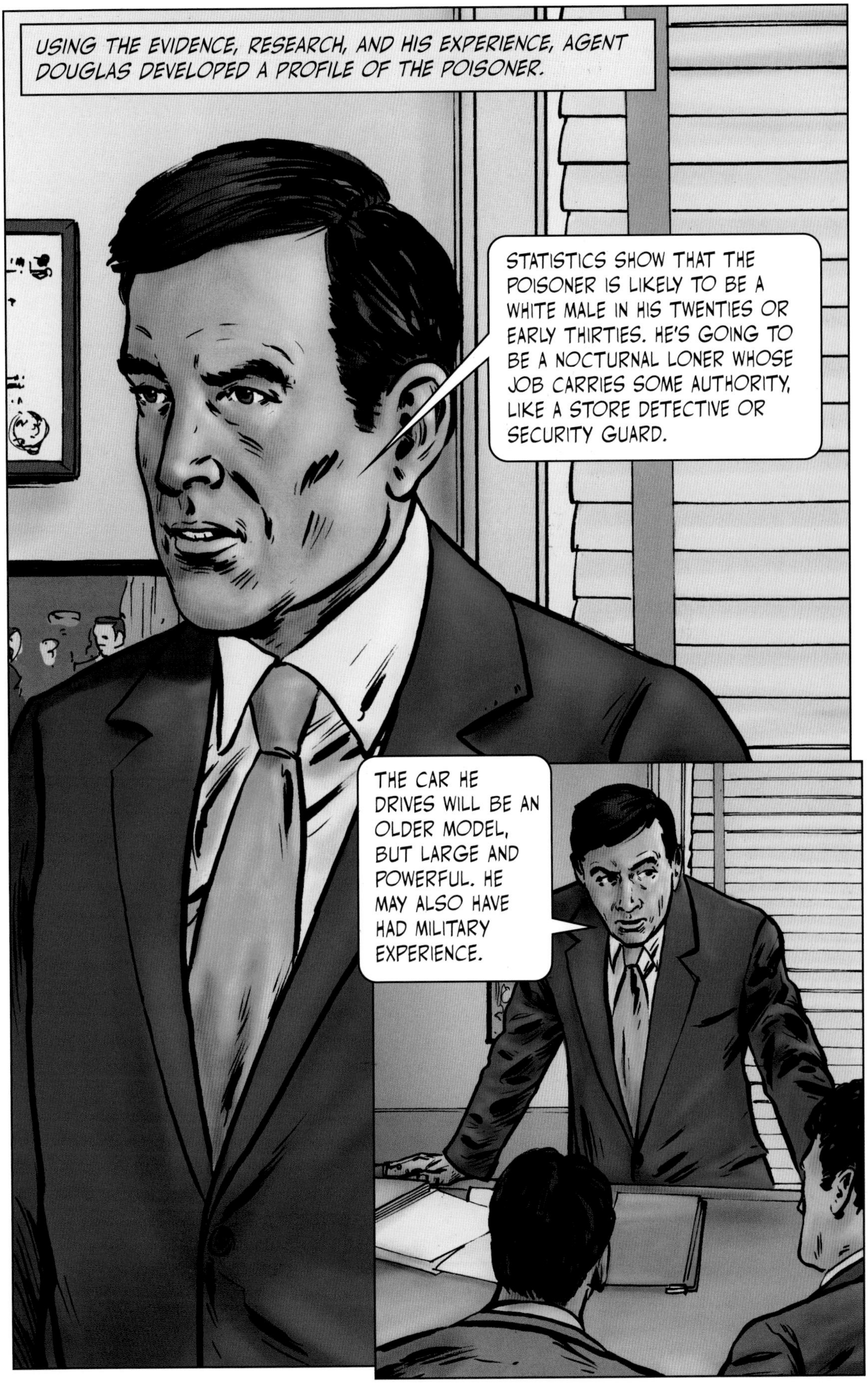
USING THE EVIDENCE, RESEARCH, AND HIS EXPERIENCE, AGENT DOUGLAS DEVELOPED A PROFILE OF THE POISONER.
STATISTICS SHOW THAT THE POISONER IS LIKELY TO BE A WHITE MALE IN HIS TWENTIES OR EARLY THIRTIES. HE'S GOING TO BE A NOCTURNAL LONER WHOSE JOB CARRIES SOME AUTHORITY, LIKE A STORE DETECTIVE OR SECURITY GUARD.
THE CAR HE DRIVES WILL BE AN OLDER MODEL, BUT LARGE AND POWERFUL. HE MAY ALSO HAVE HAD MILITARY EXPERIENCE.

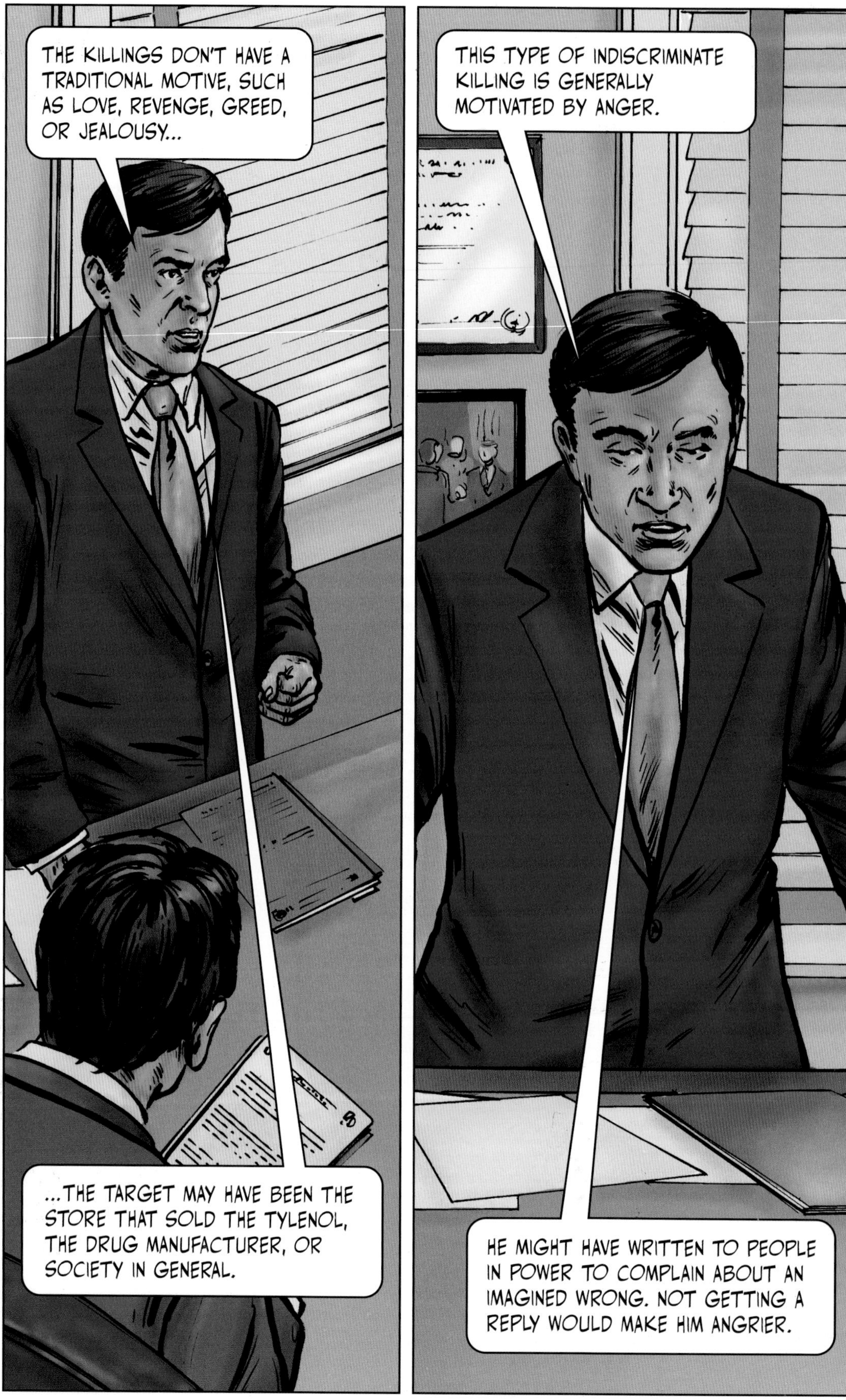
THE KILLINGS DON'T HAVE A TRADITIONAL MOTIVE, SUCH AS LOVE, REVENGE, GREED, OR JEALOUSY...
...THE TARGET MAY HAVE BEEN THE STORE THAT SOLD THE TYLENOL, THE DRUG MANUFACTURER, OR SOCIETY IN GENERAL.
THIS TYPE OF INDISCRIMINATE KILLING IS GENERALLY MOTIVATED BY ANGER.
HE MIGHT HAVE WRITTEN TO PEOPLE IN POWER TO COMPLAIN ABOUT AN IMAGINED WRONG. NOT GETTING A REPLY WOULD MAKE HIM ANGRIER.

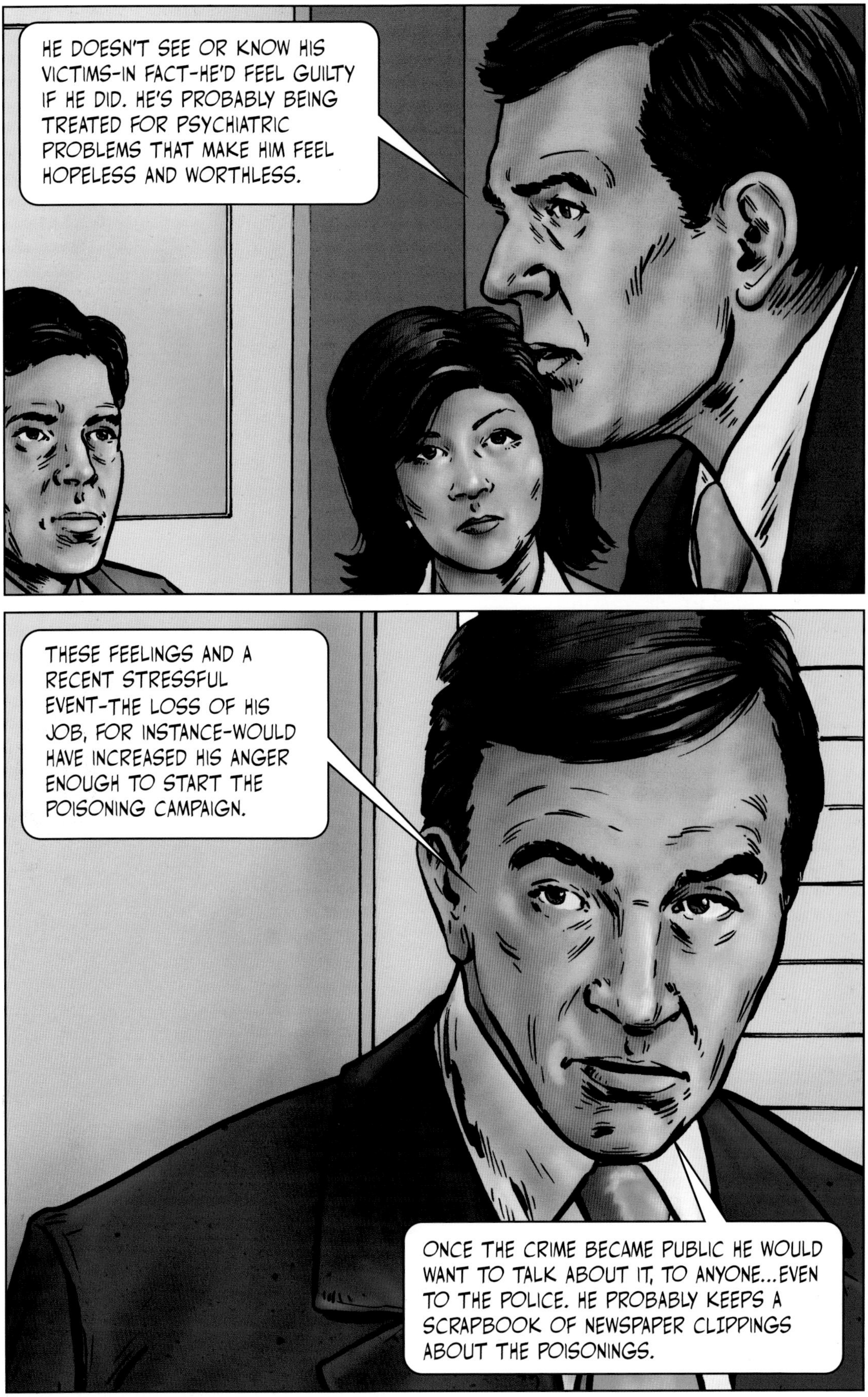
HE DOESN'T SEE OR KNOW HIS VICTIMS–IN FACT–HE'D FEEL GUILTY IF HE DID. HE'S PROBABLY BEING TREATED FOR PSYCHIATRIC PROBLEMS THAT MAKE HIM FEEL HOPELESS AND WORTHLESS.
THESE FEELINGS AND A RECENT STRESSFUL EVENT–THE LOSS OF HIS JOB, FOR INSTANCE–WOULD HAVE INCREASED HIS ANGER ENOUGH TO START THE POISONING CAMPAIGN.
ONCE THE CRIME BECAME PUBLIC HE WOULD WANT TO TALK ABOUT IT, TO ANYONE...EVEN TO THE POLICE. HE PROBABLY KEEPS A SCRAPBOOK OF NEWSPAPER CLIPPINGS ABOUT THE POISONINGS.

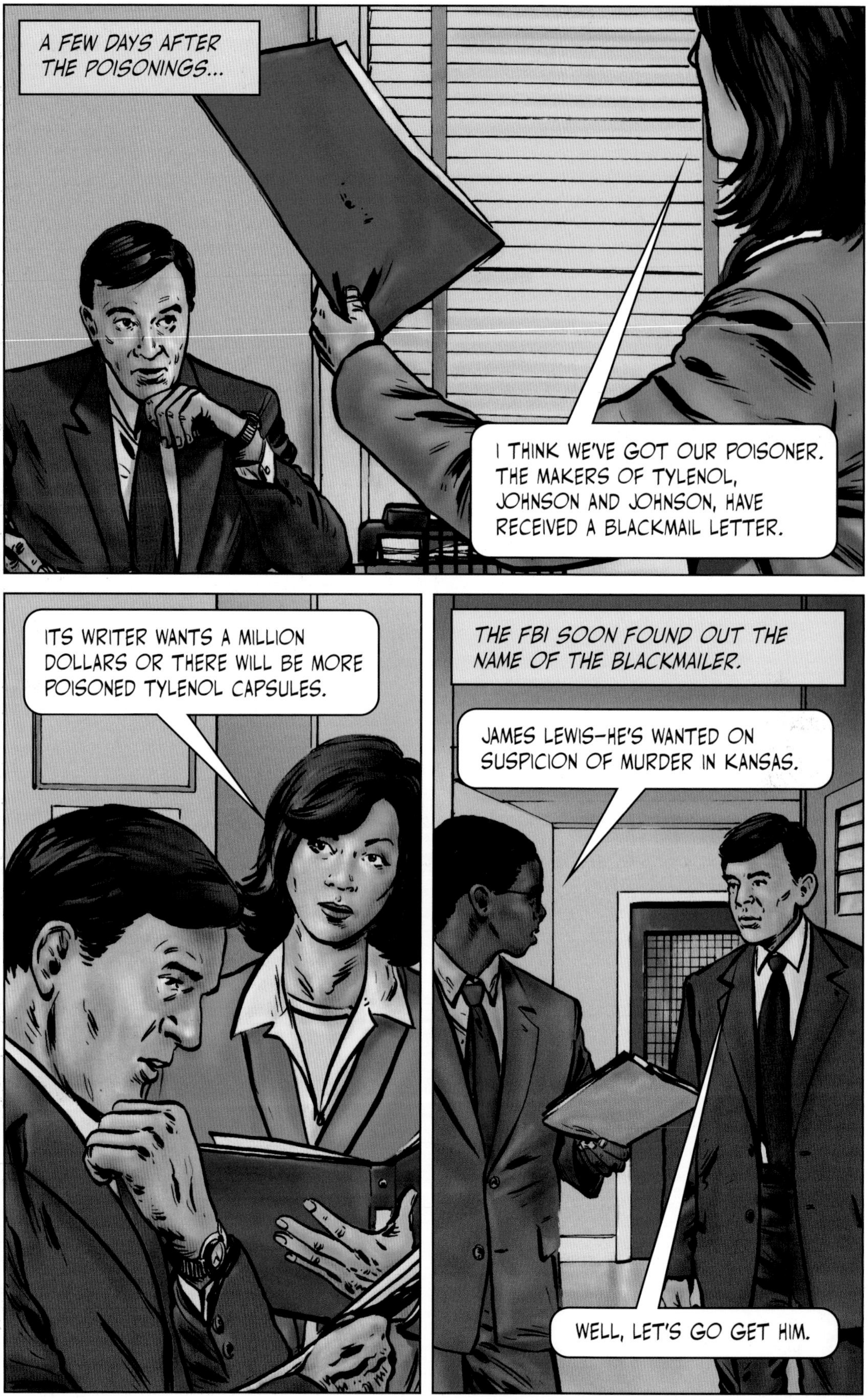
A FEW DAYS AFTER THE POISONINGS...
I THINK WE'VE GOT OUR POISONER. THE MAKERS OF TYLENOL, JOHNSON AND JOHNSON, HAVE RECEIVED A BLACKMAIL LETTER.
ITS WRITER WANTS A MILLION DOLLARS OR THERE WILL BE MORE POISONED TYLENOL CAPSULES.
THE FBI SOON FOUND OUT THE NAME OF THE BLACKMAILER.
JAMES LEWIS—HE'S WANTED ON SUSPICION OF MURDER IN KANSAS.
WELL, LET'S GO GET HIM.

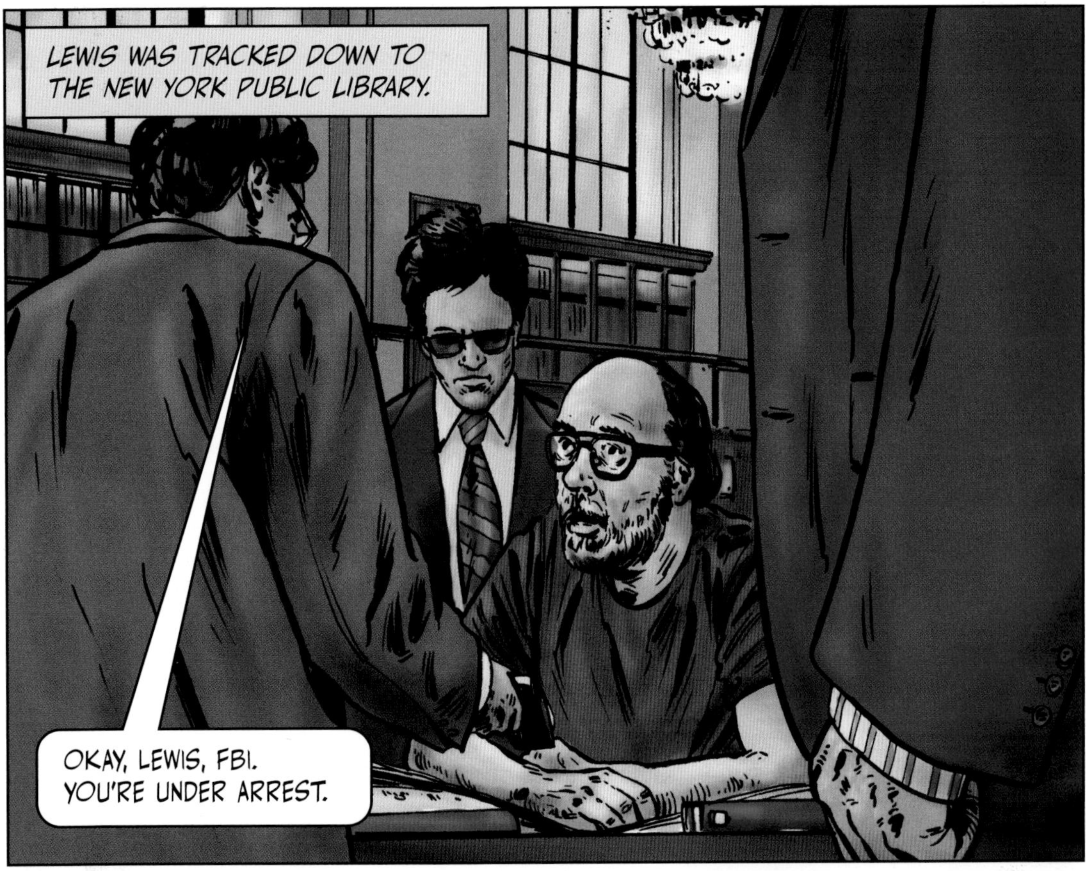
LEWIS WAS TRACKED DOWN TO THE NEW YORK PUBLIC LIBRARY.
OKAY, LEWIS, FBI. YOU'RE UNDER ARREST.

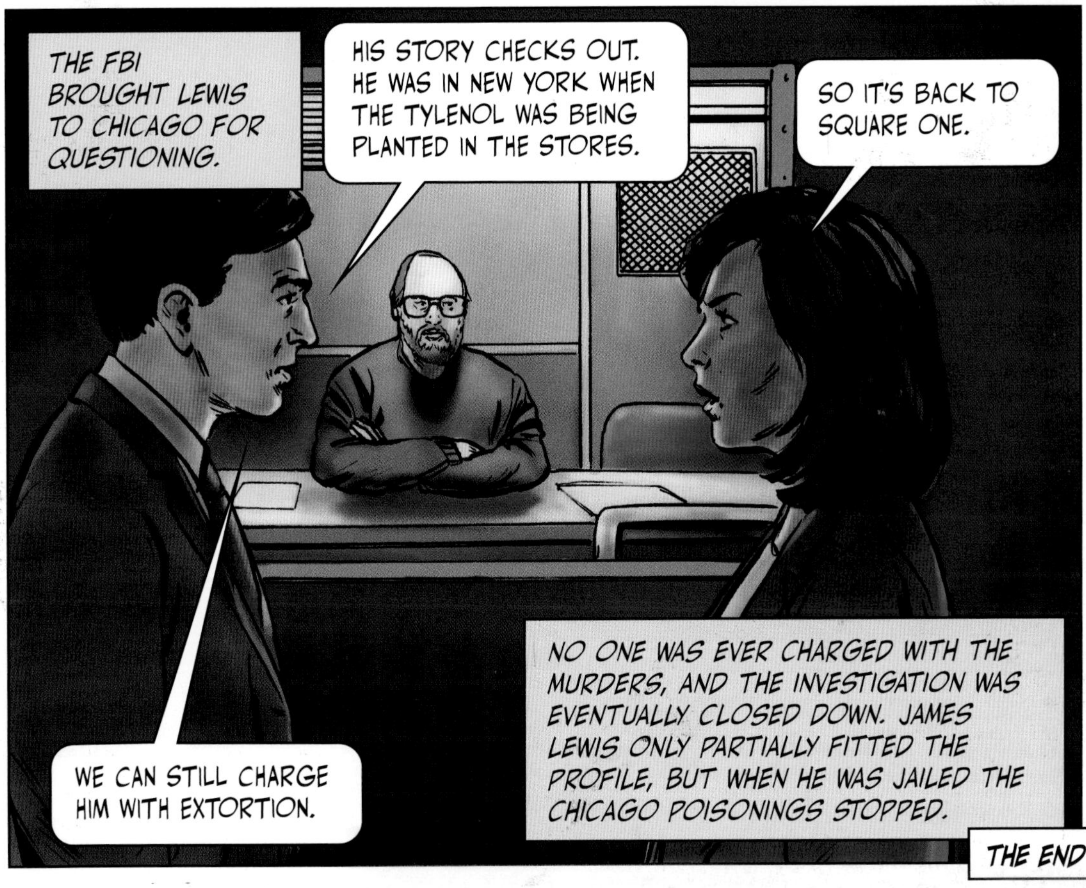
THE FBI BROUGHT LEWIS TO CHICAGO FOR QUESTIONING.
HIS STORY CHECKS OUT. HE WAS IN NEW YORK WHEN THE TYLENOL WAS BEING PLANTED IN THE STORES.
SO IT'S BACK TO SQUARE ONE.
WE CAN STILL CHARGE HIM WITH EXTORTION.
NO ONE WAS EVER CHARGED WITH THE MURDERS, AND THE INVESTIGATION WAS EVENTUALLY CLOSED DOWN. JAMES LEWIS ONLY PARTIALLY FITTED THE PROFILE, BUT WHEN HE WAS JAILED THE CHICAGO POISONINGS STOPPED.
THE END

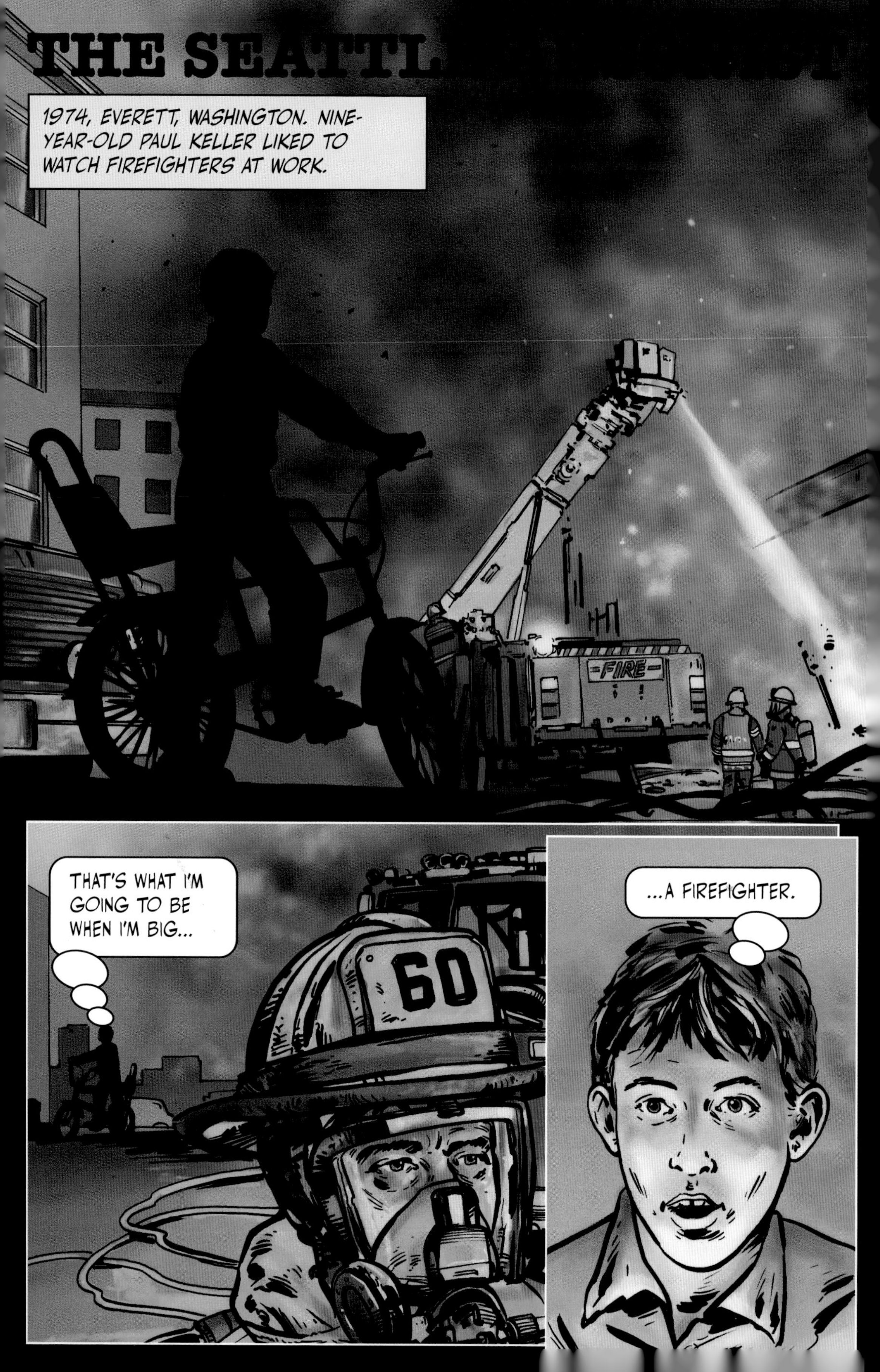
THE SEATTL
1974, EVERETT, WASHINGTON. NINE-YEAR-OLD PAUL KELLER LIKED TO WATCH FIREFIGHTERS AT WORK.
FIRE
THAT'S WHAT I'M GOING TO BE WHEN I'M BIG...
60
...A FIREFIGHTER.

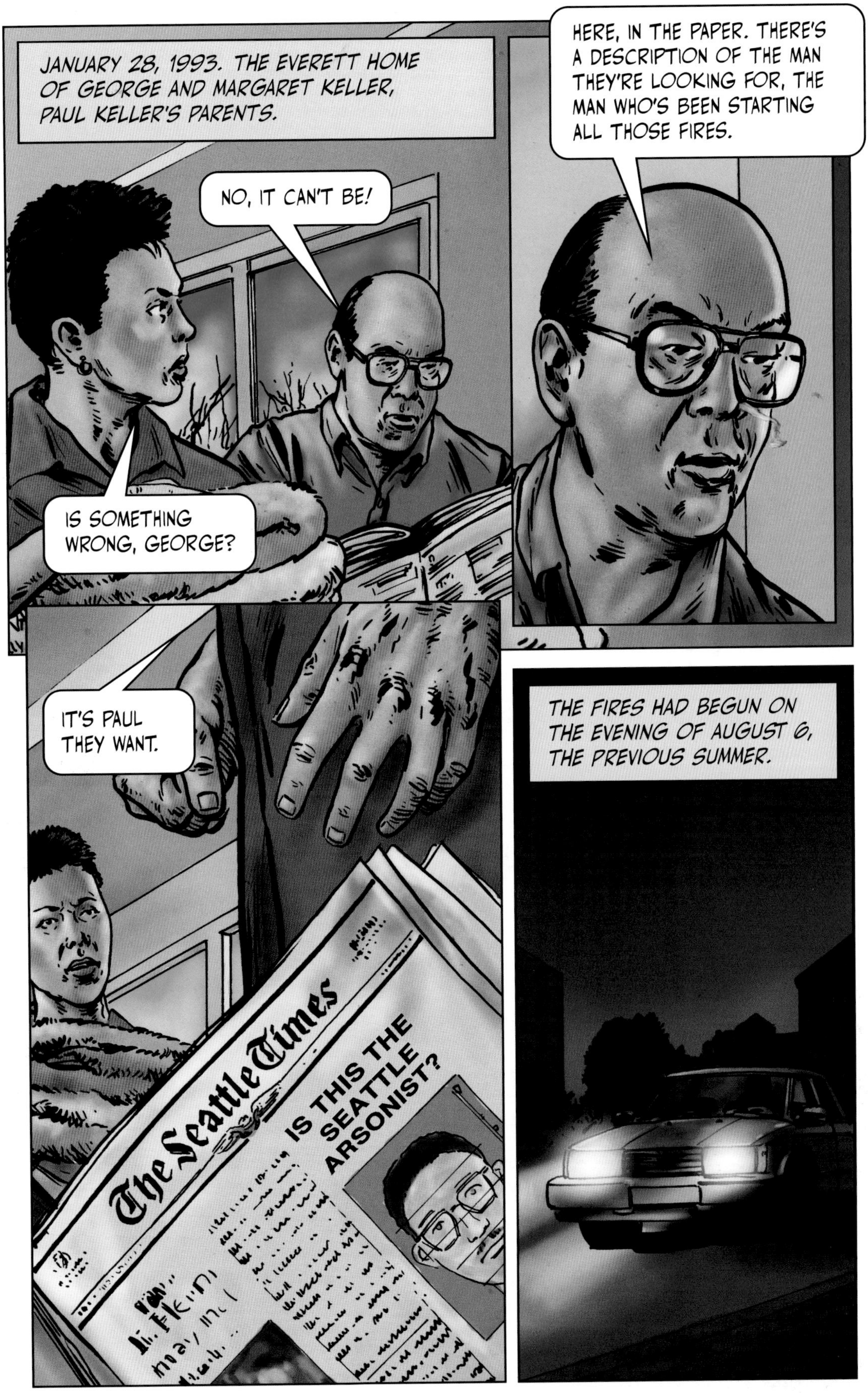
JANUARY 28, 1993. THE EVERETT HOME OF GEORGE AND MARGARET KELLER, PAUL KELLER'S PARENTS.
NO, IT CAN'T BE!
IS SOMETHING WRONG, GEORGE?
HERE, IN THE PAPER. THERE'S A DESCRIPTION OF THE MAN THEY'RE LOOKING FOR, THE MAN WHO'S BEEN STARTING ALL THOSE FIRES.
IT'S PAUL THEY WANT.
The Seattle Times
IS THIS THE SEATTLE ARSONIST?
THE FIRES HAD BEGUN ON THE EVENING OF AUGUST 6, THE PREVIOUS SUMMER.

NIGHT AFTER NIGHT, FIRES SPRANG UP IN EVERETT AND THE NEIGHBORING COUNTIES.

THE ARSONIST DID NOT PLAN THE ATTACKS...

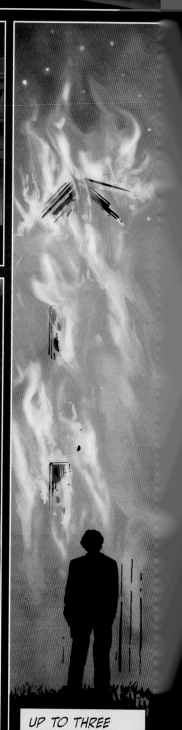

...AND USED ANYTHING CLOSE BY AS A FUEL.

UP TO THREE FIRES A NIGHT WERE STARTED.

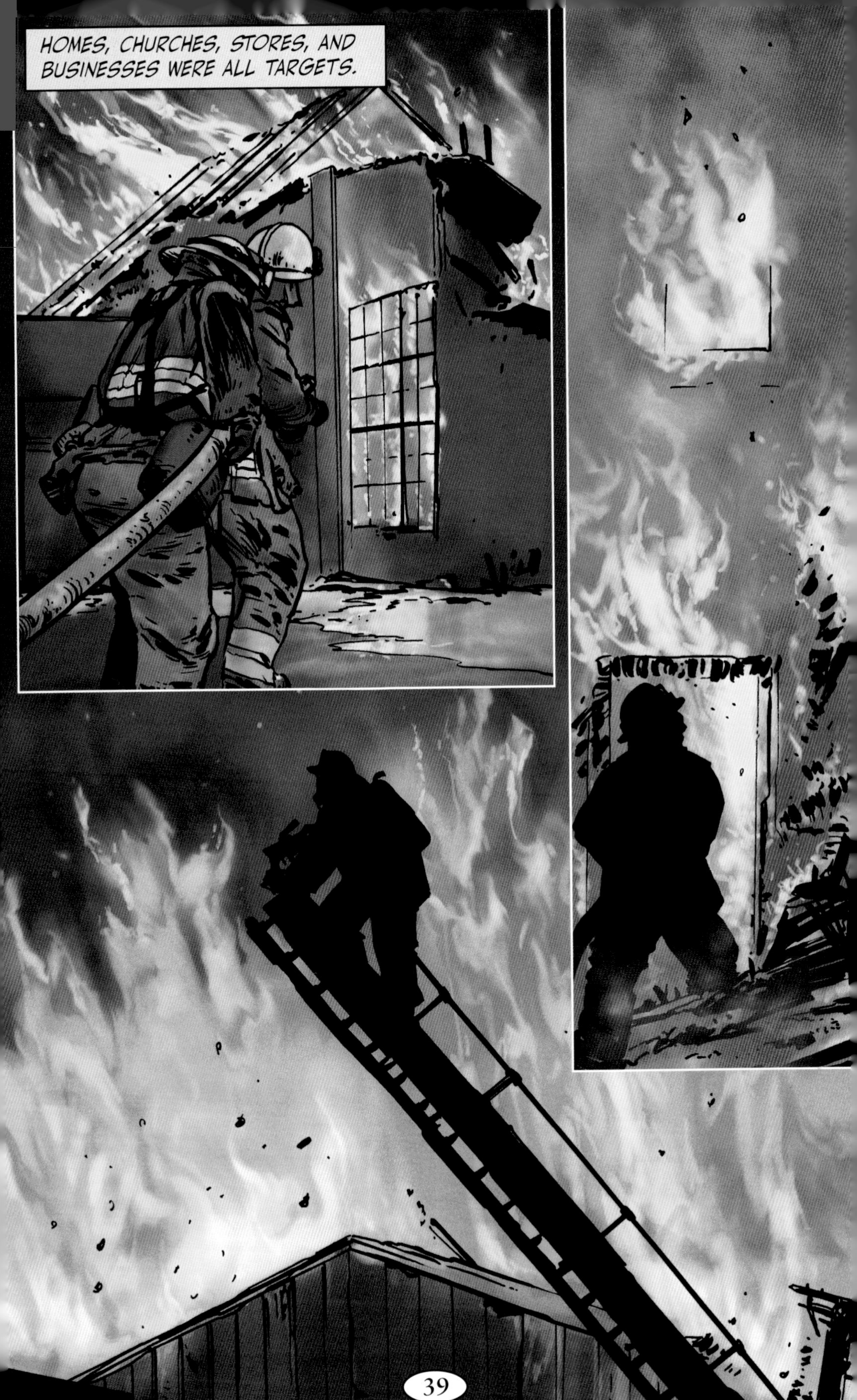
HOMES, CHURCHES, STORES, AND BUSINESSES WERE ALL TARGETS.

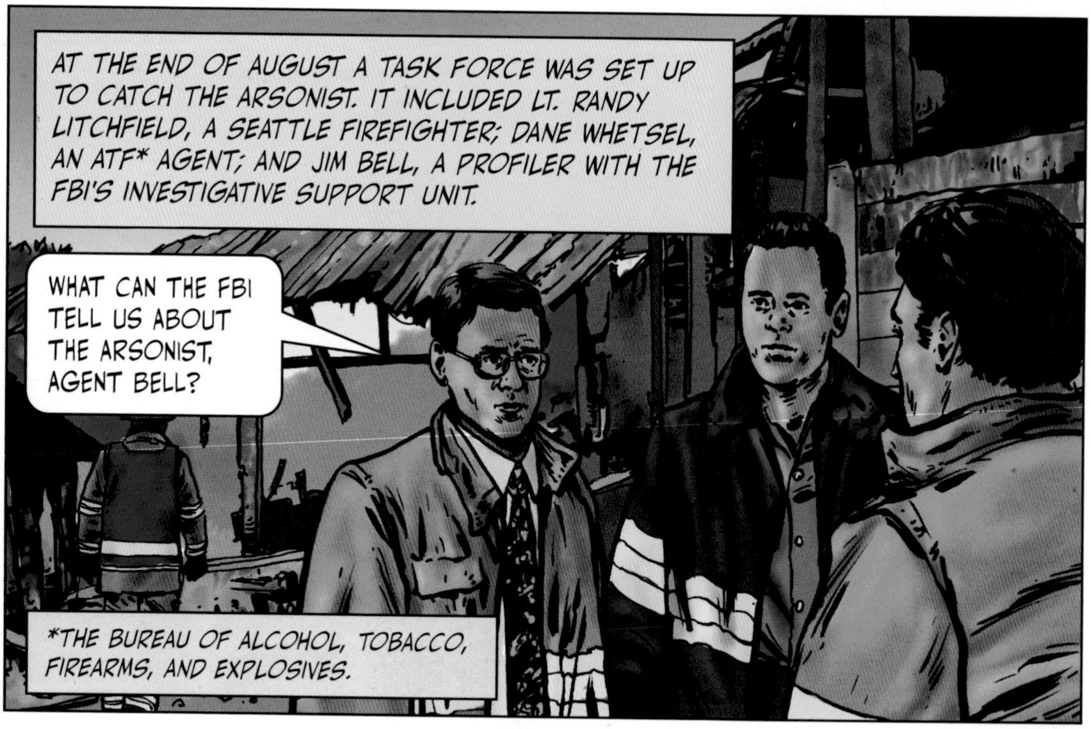
AT THE END OF AUGUST A TASK FORCE WAS SET UP TO CATCH THE ARSONIST. IT INCLUDED LT. RANDY LITCHFIELD, A SEATTLE FIREFIGHTER; DANE WHETSEL, AN ATF* AGENT; AND JIM BELL, A PROFILER WITH THE FBI'S INVESTIGATIVE SUPPORT UNIT.
WHAT CAN THE FBI TELL US ABOUT THE ARSONIST, AGENT BELL?
*THE BUREAU OF ALCOHOL, TOBACCO, FIREARMS, AND EXPLOSIVES.

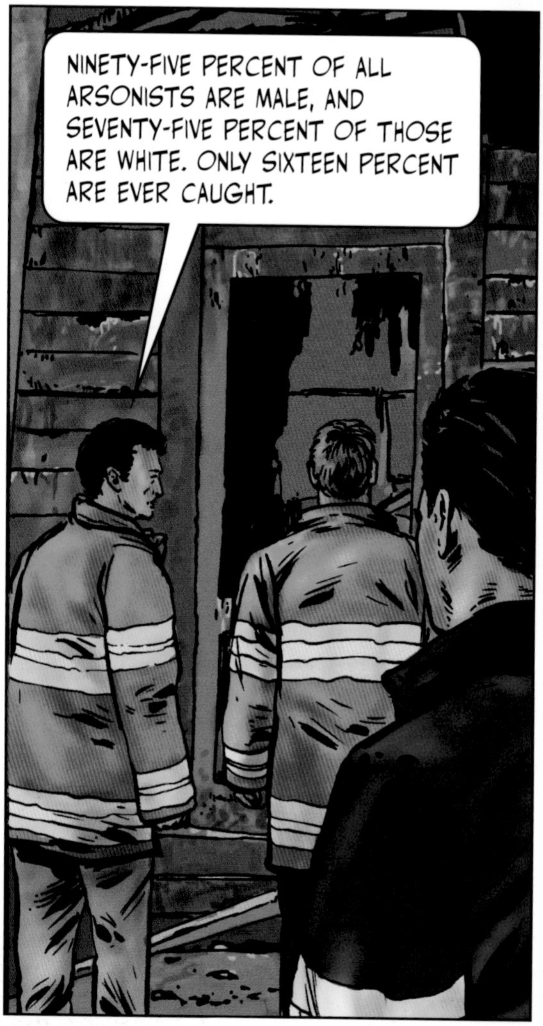
NINETY-FIVE PERCENT OF ALL ARSONISTS ARE MALE, AND SEVENTY-FIVE PERCENT OF THOSE ARE WHITE. ONLY SIXTEEN PERCENT ARE EVER CAUGHT.

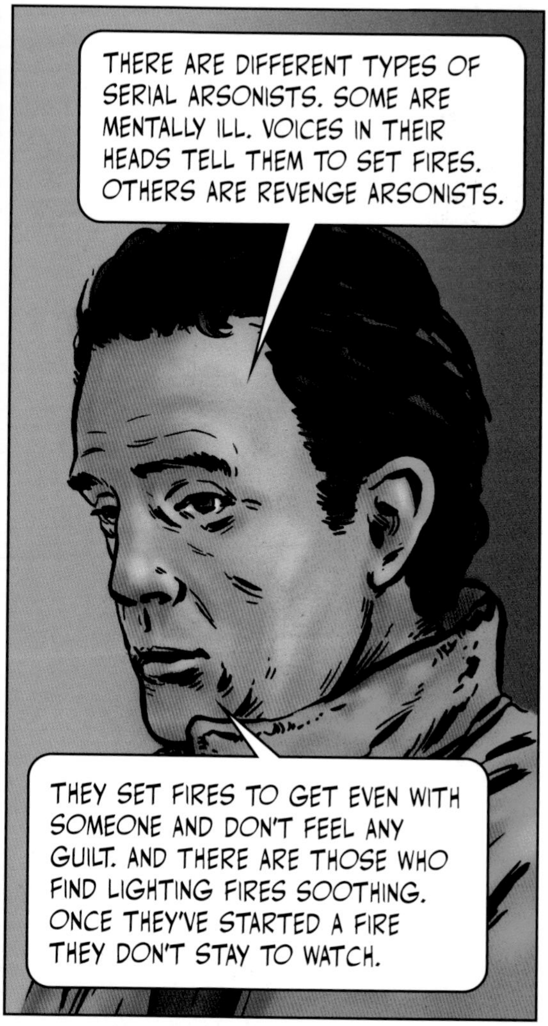
THERE ARE DIFFERENT TYPES OF SERIAL ARSONISTS. SOME ARE MENTALLY ILL. VOICES IN THEIR HEADS TELL THEM TO SET FIRES. OTHERS ARE REVENGE ARSONISTS.
THEY SET FIRES TO GET EVEN WITH SOMEONE AND DON'T FEEL ANY GUILT. AND THERE ARE THOSE WHO FIND LIGHTING FIRES SOOTHING. ONCE THEY'VE STARTED A FIRE THEY DON'T STAY TO WATCH.

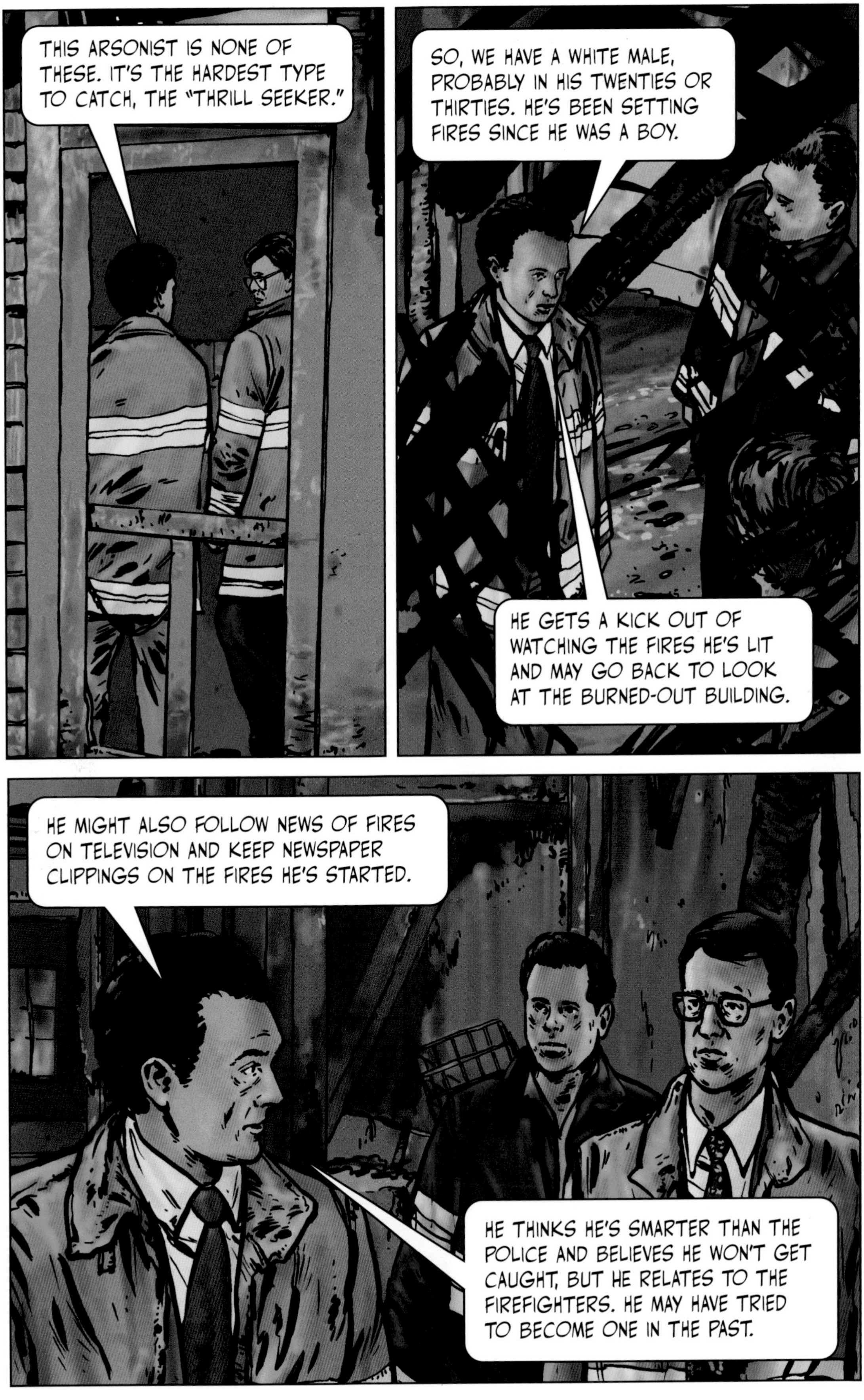
THIS ARSONIST IS NONE OF THESE. IT'S THE HARDEST TYPE TO CATCH, THE "THRILL SEEKER."
SO, WE HAVE A WHITE MALE, PROBABLY IN HIS TWENTIES OR THIRTIES. HE'S BEEN SETTING FIRES SINCE HE WAS A BOY.
HE GETS A KICK OUT OF WATCHING THE FIRES HE'S LIT AND MAY GO BACK TO LOOK AT THE BURNED-OUT BUILDING.
HE MIGHT ALSO FOLLOW NEWS OF FIRES ON TELEVISION AND KEEP NEWSPAPER CLIPPINGS ON THE FIRES HE'S STARTED.
HE THINKS HE'S SMARTER THAN THE POLICE AND BELIEVES HE WON'T GET CAUGHT, BUT HE RELATES TO THE FIREFIGHTERS. HE MAY HAVE TRIED TO BECOME ONE IN THE PAST.

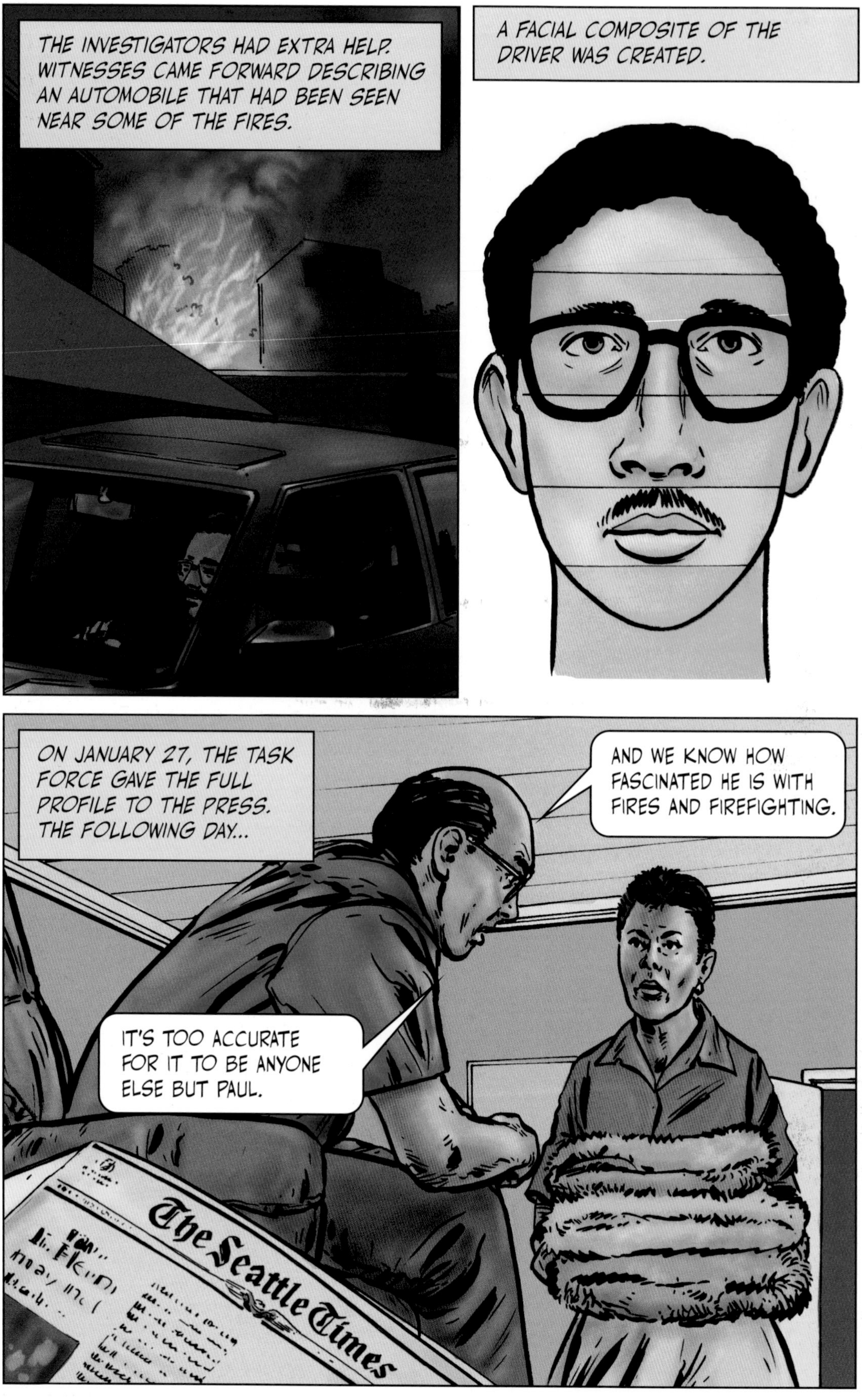
THE INVESTIGATORS HAD EXTRA HELP. WITNESSES CAME FORWARD DESCRIBING AN AUTOMOBILE THAT HAD BEEN SEEN NEAR SOME OF THE FIRES.
A FACIAL COMPOSITE OF THE DRIVER WAS CREATED.
ON JANUARY 27, THE TASK FORCE GAVE THE FULL PROFILE TO THE PRESS. THE FOLLOWING DAY...
AND WE KNOW HOW FASCINATED HE IS WITH FIRES AND FIREFIGHTING.
IT'S TOO ACCURATE FOR IT TO BE ANYONE ELSE BUT PAUL.
The Seattle Times

WHAT ARE WE GOING TO DO, GEORGE?

THERE'S ONLY ONE THING WE CAN DO.

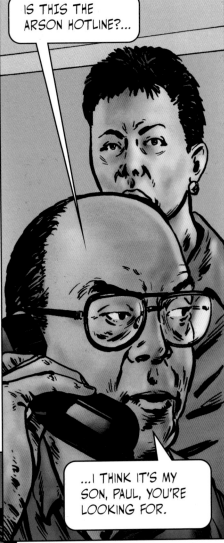

IS THIS THE ARSON HOTLINE?...

...I THINK IT'S MY SON, PAUL, YOU'RE LOOKING FOR.

6:30 A.M., FEBRUARY 6, PAUL KELLER'S APARTMENT...

YOU HAVE THE RIGHT TO REMAIN SILENT...

AT HIS TRIAL, PAUL KELLER ADMITTED TO SETTING 64 FIRES AND CAUSING $16,000,000 WORTH OF DAMAGE. HE WAS SENTENCED TO 75 YEARS IN PRISON. IN MARCH 1994 KELLER WAS FOUND GUILTY OF MURDER. THREE OCCUPANTS OF A RETIREMENT HOME HAD DIED IN A 1993 FIRE THAT HE HAD STARTED. HE WAS SENTENCED TO 99 YEARS. INVESTIGATORS BELIEVE THAT KELLER IS RESPONSIBLE FOR MANY MORE FIRES AND MORE DEATHS.

THE END

OTHER FAMOUS CASES

Here are some more celebrated cases that feature criminal profiling.

JACK THE RIPPER

Mary Ann Nichols's body was found on August 31, 1888, in Whitechapel, a poor area of Victorian London. Her throat had

been cut. Over the next eleven weeks four more women were murdered in the same way. The newspapers called the murderer Jack the Ripper, a name that stuck. One of the police surgeons on the case was Dr. Thomas Bond. He became particularly interested in why the women had been killed in such a violent manner. He reconstructed the crimes and carefully looked at the evidence, trying to understand what the Ripper was like as a person. Dr. Bond's conclusions helped create the very first criminal profile. Jack the Ripper was never caught so we do not know how close Dr. Bond's profile came to the truth.

THE ZODIAC KILLER

Between 1968 and 1969 five people were murdered in the San Francisco area of California. Two others were attacked but survived. The killer wrote coded letters to the press taunting the police. It was through these letters that the killer got his name, "The Zodiac." A profile was written. It said that The Zodiac was someone who wanted to be in charge. He was a person who liked to exercise control over his victims and the authorities. To him murder was a game. Despite all the police's efforts, The Zodiac Killer was never caught.

David Meirhofer

The FBI's Behavioral Science Unit (see page 6) had been in operation for only a year when it received its first case. In June 1973, a young girl had been abducted from a Montana campsite. Agents Howard Teten and Patrick Mullany wrote a profile for the offender. They believed the culprit to be a young, white male who was excited by his crimes. He was someone who liked to take away a souvenir from his victim. The profile helped lead the police to 23-year-old David Meirhofer. Starting in 1966, Meirhofer had killed four people, including the kidnapped girl. At his home the police found souvenirs from all of them. David Meirhofer became the first serial killer to be caught by the FBI using their new profiling methods.

The Unabomber

Campus police officer Terry Marker had been lucky. His left hand had been only slightly injured when the poorly made bomb exploded. A package containing the bomb had been sent to Professor Buckley Crist at Northwestern University, in Illinois. He became suspicious and gave it to Marker. It was May 1978, and this was the first of sixteen bombs that would leave three dead and twenty-three wounded over the next eighteen years. When, in 1979, the bomber almost succeeded in blowing up a Boeing 727 in mid-flight, the FBI was called in. They code-named him UNABOM, University and Airline bomber. John Douglas of the FBI's Behavioral Science Unit developed a profile. He thought the bomber was a scruffy male who had academic qualifications but who hated modern technology. In 1996 David Kaczynski contacted the police, saying he thought that his brother Theodore was the bomber. The FBI found Theodore Kaczynski in an untidy Montana cabin surrounded by bomb parts. He was a math professor once, but had given it up to live a simple life in the woods.

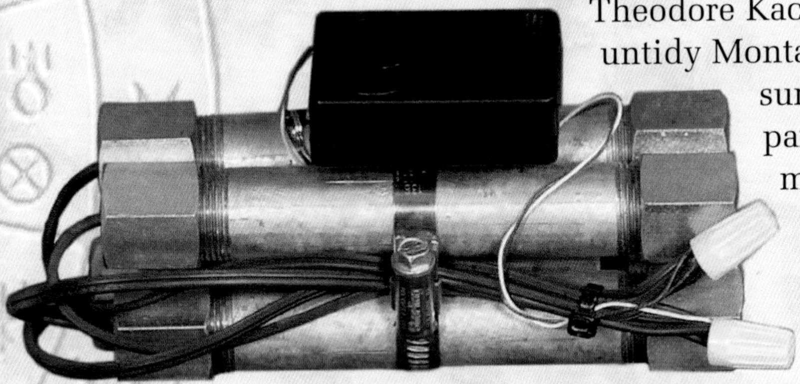

GLOSSARY

academic A lecturer or scholar who works at a university or college.

archives Places where past documents and records are stored.

capsule A small pill containing medicine.

conclusions Decisions arrived at through reasoning.

coroner A court official who investigates murders and violent deaths.

culprit A person who has committed a crime.

dastardly Referring to something or someone that is evil and cruel.

employee Someone who works for a business or organization.

extortion Trying to get money through the use of threats and force.

grudge Prolonged ill feelings held by someone toward another person or organization.

mocked Made fun of someone.

nocturnal Awake during the night and asleep during the day.

phrases Small groups of words that form short sayings and expressions.

potassium cyanide An extremely poisonous white compound.

provoke To set off a strong reaction in someone.

psychiatrist A doctor who specializes in treating mental illness.

qualifications The documented proof of professional achievemen.

reconstructed Reenacted an event.

relates Feels sympathy and understanding for someone or something.

society A community of people who live together.

souvenir Something that is kept or taken from a place as a reminder or trophy.

suburbs The neighborhoods that surround a city or large town.

tactic A plan used to achieve a goal.

tampered Interfered with.

warrant A legal document that allows court officials to carry out individual court orders.

FOR MORE INFORMATION

ORGANIZATIONS

American Academy of Forensic Sciences
410 North 21st Street
Colorado Springs, CO 80904
(719) 636-1100
Web site: http://www.aafs.org

The American College of Forensic Examiners
Institute of Forensic Science
2750 East Sunshine Street
Springfield, MO 65804
(417) 881-3818
Web site: http://www.acfei.com

FOR FURTHER READING

Balcavage, Dynise. *The Federal Bureau of Investigation.* New York, NY: Facts on File, 2000.

Davis, Mary. *Working in Law and Justice.* Minneapolis, MN: Lerner Publications, 1999.

Kobilinsky, Lawrence, Ph.D., Series editor. *Inside Forensic Science.* New York, NY: Chelsea House Publishers, 2005.

Streissguth, Thomas. *International Terrorists.* Minneapolis, MN: Oliver Press, 1993.

INDEX

Web Sites

Due to the changing nature of Internet links, Rosen Publishing has developed an online list of Web sites related to the subject of this book. This site is updated regularly. Please use this link to access the list:

http://www.rosenlinks.com/gfs/sccp